THE KINDNESS OF RANDOM STRANGERS
Hitchhiking San Diego to Panama - 1961

by

Carl J Stephani
Marilyn C Stephani

Copyright 2018© Marilyn and Carl Stephani, all rights reserved. No part of this book may be used or reproduced in any manner whatsoever without written permission except in the case of brief quotations embodied in critical articles and reviews. For information address: 5505 East 110th Place, Tulsa, OK 74137. This book is based on a true incident. The conversations were produced based on best memory and notes in the journals of the three travelers.

ACKNOWLEDGMENTS

This book is intended as a small token of appreciation for all those who helped Fred, Ross and me live through the adventure it describes. Unfortunately, because we did not keep more detailed journals, there are many who helped us whose names we no longer have.

For my part I especially want to thank Fred Ryan and Ross Barber with whom I experienced this adventure, for their kindness in sharing their journals with me when I finally got around to taking the time to write the story down. They are a couple of very valued old friends.

Although others were instrumental in making this trip a success, it should be understood that all the opinions, perspectives, ideas, thoughts and interpretations expressed in this book are fully and completely those of the authors.

Ross, Carl, and Fred in Pacific Beach, California, a year after THE TRIP

DEDICATION

This book is dedicated to Fred Ryan, Ross Barber, and Ransome Wyman who helped make THE TRIP happen; and to our grandchildren and their grandchildren who may someday enjoy knowing what it was like for a couple of *norteamericano* college kids to travel on a shoestring from San Diego, California, to Panama and back in the early 1960s.

CHAPTER 1 - HIGH SCHOOL

"Youth is the best time to be rich, and the best time to be poor."
Euripides, Greek poet and dramatist

I was tall for my age - six foot four inches by the time I was a freshman in high school, although I only weighed 168 pounds. My height made people think I would be good in athletics, but I didn't have enough coordination to be very good. I liked playing basketball and football because it seemed like it would enhance my standing with girls, but it really never seemed to work that way for me.

In my senior year we were the first players in the school to get face guards put on our leather football helmets; one bar in front of our teeth. In the off season I jogged to try to keep in shape.

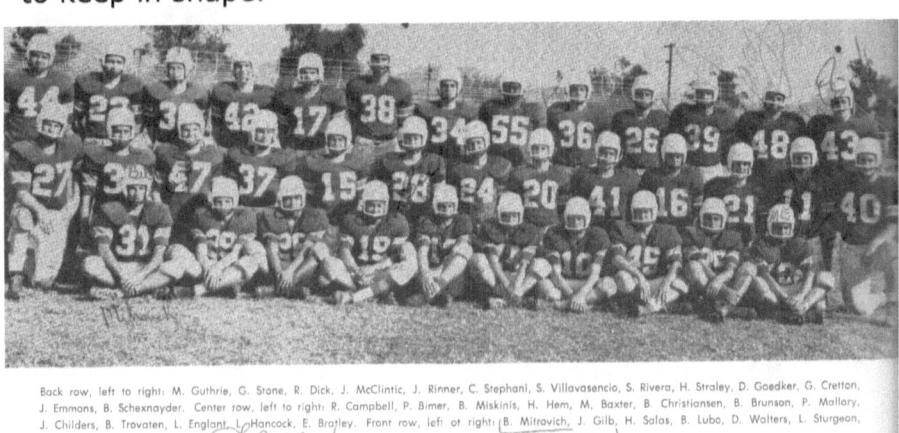

Stephani #38, back row, middle

In high school I kept my hair in a flat top which my father cut, and I cut his hair, because we both thought that paying for haircuts was not the best way to spend our money.

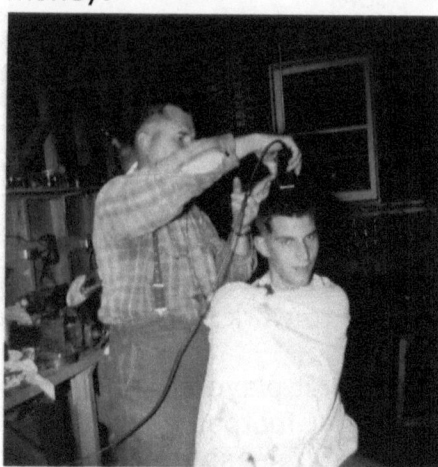
"Pop" cutting Carl's hair

Carl cutting Pop's hair

I was pretty bright, and for the first several years of high school I was at the head of my class. There were about 350 kids in my class. During the summer between my junior and senior years I took a typing course and, because my coordination wasn't all that good, I got my first and only "C" grade in high school in that course. That gave Fred the lead over me.

Fred was probably my best friend in high school. He transferred in during our junior year. He had played two years of football in his former high schools, but had to stop playing when he came to El Cajon because he had no choice but to work a lot after school to help make ends meet. He had also been very active in student government at his former high schools - he went to four different high schools because of his family's instability - and was elected president of his class twice before he got to El Cajon.

We had a lot in common in that regard; my senior year I had been president of my class.

Ross

Although Fred was not able to be active in sports and student government because of his family finances, he was always just very smart. It used to always gripe me, though, that he graduated as our class valedictorian instead of me all because of a "C" grade I got in a summer school typing course that I didn't even need to take! As I recall, Ross graduated third in our class, and we all decided to go to the University of California at Riverside (UCR).

Carl & Fred

Among other things, Fred was assigned the job of designing a new sign for our high school in our senior year. In his yearbook I wrote that he did a "bang up job" on the new school sign, and I added, "it was the most banged up sign I ever saw!" That last bit was intended to make Fred laugh, and I think actually it did. Sometimes I said things that made Ross laugh too.

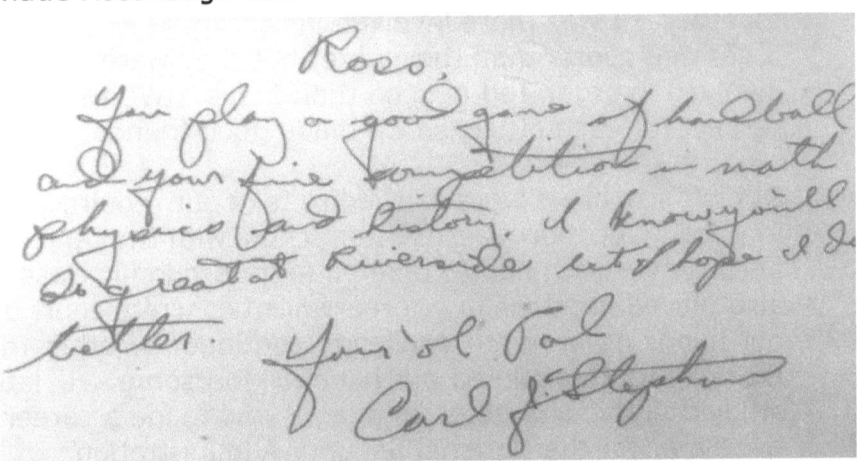

Carl's note to Ross in his 1959 high school annual: "Ross, You play a good game of handball and your [sic] fine competition in math, physics, and history. I know you'll do great at Riverside but I hope I do better. Your 'ol Pal, Carl"

I was raised in an atheistic family; I always had the impression that Ross' family was very religious. Ross got Fred interested in his religion; Fred joined Ross' church group, and the two of them were very strongly in agreement on that subject throughout our school years.

Ross was physically able but never played organized sports that I knew of. He was stockier than Fred or I, but we were all pretty good looking. I was the tallest; Fred and Ross were about the same height. To me, Fred had the look of a light skinned part-native American (although he insisted he didn't have any native American blood in him); Ross looked to me like Mister Rogers. I was tall and lanky with sharp features and a chin that came to a point like Kirk Douglas.

We helped each other in our high school studies, even though we had a moderately strong friendly competition for grades. We liked each other and never had a serious personal argument that I can remember. We were all philosophically minded, so we took the vicissitudes of life with some grace and had a pretty enjoyable time whenever we were together. I was more involved in

Kirk Douglas

organized sports than they were; but they were more involved in organized religion than I was. We all had respect for each other, so we made good friends.

In high school we were allowed to take our required Physical Education classes after school with the tennis team because we each had to take an extra academic class. We also played handball in a three-walled concrete court until our hands ds were too swollen to continue. Another friend, Frank Vittor, completed our handball foursome. He later studied Arabic and other languages and made a career as a translator for the National Security Administration.

Sometimes we jogged together on the school track, and we went snorkeling for abalone off La Jolla Shores a couple of times.

Ross came from a very stable family, so he always had a little less at risk than Fred. Fred's folks were divorced, which was considered a real tragedy in those days, and his family wasn't able to concentrate on him as much as Ross's family and my family were able to concentrate on us.

Snorkeling with stylish spear fishing gear off La Jolla Shores in 1958

Ross and I were the only boys in our families; Fred had two younger brothers, one younger sister, and two older sisters.

My family had moved around a lot because my father wanted to retrace the travels across the continent that he had made as a boy with his father. I didn't know it at the time, but during those travels he was actually always searching for his father who had abandoned him and his mother at the Long Beach, California, train station in the summer of 1920. My father was born on Monday, July 22, 1912 in New York City. I don't know the exact date my grandfather left him in 1920 but I know he was 8 years old.

To make our family's trips from 1952 to 1954 our family of five (me and my two sisters and parents) lived in a thirty-three foot long Spartan aluminum trailer which we towed with our 1950 gray Nash Ambassador.

The Stephani family's 33' Spartan aluminum trailer

The Stephani family's 1950 Nash Ambassador

Forty years after our cross country travels were over we learned what had happened to "Grandpa Joe", but that was twenty years after he had died, so my father never got to see his father again after 1920.

My father - we called him "Pop" - was a good father to me; he taught me how to hunt, fish, and fix cars and things, and that gave me strong feelings of self-reliance.

When I got my turn to get out into the world, I thought I could do anything, and I didn't think I needed anybody's help. Fred and Ross were pretty self-assured too; they had their religion and its members behind them wherever they went.

Carl and Pop rebuilding the 1950 Nash Ambassador rear-end someplace along the way in Indiana - that rear-end was never designed to pull a 33' long trailer

Family portrait, Old Tucson, 1952, left to right: Carol, Mom Louise, Diane, "Big" paternal grandmother Mary Sedlacek, Pop Charlie, Carl

Carl practicing hunting skills - 1949

CHAPTER 2 - COLLEGE

> "When they are learned, they think they are wise..."
> 2 Nephi 9:28, <u>Book</u> <u>of</u> <u>Mormon</u>

I began college as a math major, with a Russian minor. Fred also started out taking math and Russian, so we had courses together.

Carl and Fred studying at college in Riverside, California

Fred and Ross shared a dormitory room. Ross wasn't in any classes with Fred and me; he was doing his own academic thing, I think it was in biology. His parents ran an old folks home which he was probably going to inherit, so he didn't have to worry so much about what he studied.

I thought I was a math wizard when I graduated from high school because I had won a new fiberglass slide rule in a San Diego County-wide math contest sponsored by Convair Aeronautics. My first semester in calculus, however, showed me that either San Diego County didn't have much going for it in the way of math teachers, or I just wasn't very bright, because - compared to most of the other math students in my college class - I didn't know diddly-squat about mathematics. By my sophomore year I realized I wasn't ever going to catch up in calculus, and I was doing fairly well in Russian. Fred found himself in a similar situation so at that point we both became Russian majors. Ross had the same problem with calculus. After his Freshman year he switched his major from pre-med to music. When he graduated he had a botany major with a minor in music. Ross had studied Spanish in high school and took two years of German in college.

I played football my freshman year in college, but I wasn't really a football player. I was long and lanky and not very aggressive, but I wanted girls to like me so I figured I'd better do something besides reading esoteric books like Erasmus' In Praise of Folly in the downtown bus station (which I did) to attract their attention. Basically I saw myself as a kind of an intellectual mystic, so some evenings I would walk downtown and read books in unusual places - like the old Mission Hotel - but that wasn't too effective in attracting intelligent, articulate, pretty-looking girls, so I also went out for Football.

The football team at the University of California at Riverside in 1959 was not a very successful team. We played the inmates at Chino State Penitentiary once and came away with three guys with broken bones. I didn't play my sophomore year; no one asked me to, and I wasn't attracting much attention sitting on the bench until the last few minutes of the game when all the scrubs were put in.

Ross, Fred and I spent countless hours discussing religion and why, how, what if .... I was fascinated by the idea of existence, and we had lots of time together because, in addition to our classes, Fred (who was completely self-supporting) and I also washed dishes and mopped floors in the dormitory cafeteria for our money to stay in college.

I had studied Spanish for three years in high school. My sophomore year in college I also enrolled in a German course, and second semester I got into an introductory French course. Fred took one semester of French at UCR.

Sophomore year all three of us moved out of the dormitories into apartments. There I met Ransome Wyman and John Laudenschlager. They were science majors.

John was from San Diego; Ransome from the L.A. area. John was shorter than the rest of us. He was a very solid guy from a regular middle-class family whose father had been in the military; he wasn't too witty, or cynical, or sarcastic like the rest of us college kids liked to

Ransome Wyman - my only photo of this great guy!

be; he was just very down to earth. We liked to call him "Mr. Clean." Ransome's parents were Nazarene missionaries in British Honduras, now known as Belize.

Ransome was a total free spirit. He was a handsome guy with a very neatly kept pompadour haircut. He could laugh along with the best of us, and he was very sharp witted. He knew he didn't want anything to do with

John Laudenschlager another great guy!

religion, neither for or against, and that he was going to be a chemist. He wanted to make a lot of money and enjoy life. Ransome didn't talk very much about his parents. He got an apartment that year with Roger Cude, another chemist, who also became a good friend.

Roger Cude - what a totally cheerful friend!

Roger was also from well-adjusted middle-class family and had been raised in the San Gabriel area of Los Angeles. He was fairly skinny and had a pretty bad case of acne a lot of the time, but he was a heckuva friendly guy, and super nice to everyone. He was a math genius and had a terrific sense of humor. He would laugh at anything, and really give it his best whenever anyone told a joke or anything. We all had good senses of humor, but Roger's was the best.

Roger didn't drink much at all, none of us did; and Ross and Fred were teetotalers because of their religion. None of us smoked because we didn't have that kind of money. Once in a while one of us would buy a cheap cigar or two and then we would smoke them (except Fred and Ross), but otherwise we were a pretty clean group. All of us had old fashioned morals as far as girls were concerned; although we all liked kissing girls as much as any college guys do.

In the Spring of 1961 the guys and I got to talking about what to do during the summer between sophomore and junior years. I was going to have some money left at the end of the semester and I didn't have a particularly specific girl friend at the time. Fred was beginning to get serious with one girl he was spending time with, and Ross had a girl he spent a lot of time with also, although not enough to pass up an opportunity to see some interesting parts of the world.

I had visited Tijuana, Mexico, with my folks several times and we had lots of fun there. I still have the picture of my two aunts from Brooklyn on a wagon with a zebra-painted donkey in front. I had fond memories of Mexico as I knew it.

Zebra-striped donkey, Pop, family friend, Aunt Stephanie, Aunt Josie, "Little Stephanie," Mom in Tijuana 1960

As something to do for the summer, I mentioned Mexico because of the money-stretching we could do there. Then there were the pyramids; maybe we could even go on to Central America - then, "heck, why not?- let's hitch-hike to Panama!"

At first the idea was just a joke among us, whenever we couldn't think of any other conversation - "Hey, you getting ready for THE TRIP?..." "How much money you going to have for THE TRIP?.." "What do your folks think about THE

TRIP?..." It was just a joke for a while, but then the more we joked about it the more it got into our minds.

Ransome made it all a pretty serious when he and John Laudenschlager actually definitely decided to visit Ransome's folks that summer. We all talked about the jungles, the canal, the Mexican food and the beaches but at the end of the semester nothing specific had come of the discussion for the rest of us. We all went home and forgot about traveling for a few days.

By the time sophomore year was over we were all pretty tired - especially me, Fred and Ross. Ransome had some kind of cushy job in a chemistry lab that paid him lots to do almost nothing so he wasn't worn out; but I was carrying a full load of course work, and my sophomore year, besides the cafeteria clean-up, I also got a job in the language lab, changing tapes in the machines and checking people in and out, and a job operating the projector for an art class on film.

1951 Rambler Convertible

I drove a 1951 Rambler convertible that my father and I had spray painted white at home with the air compressor he had made. I took all the carpets out of the car sanded the metal to remove the rust, prepped it with "Metal Prep", and then undercoated the bare metal. I bought some baby blue carpet remnants and, while the undercoat was still wet, I stuck the carpet down on it. It really looked neat and the undercoat helped to make the car a lot quieter. Once the carpeting was in I drove the car down to Tijuana and had upholstery made for it and a new top put on it. It was quite a hot little Nash

1961 Corvette

Rambler convertible, as far as little Nash Rambler convertibles go; however, it was not as hot as, say, a Corvette.

Fred drove a 1951 gray Studebaker that looked about as unique as a car could look, but it ran well. Fred's car didn't really compete with a Corvette either. As I recall, in those days Ross didn't have a car.

1951 Studebaker Coupe

I dated several girls my freshman and sophomore years, but I didn't really get serious with any of them. The closest I came to getting serious was with a girl in my Russian class. We drove over to Manhattan Beach once on a date and stayed at the apartment of one of Ransome's friends. We had a wild time by the standards of those days. We drank beer and spent the evening on the beach until about 1 AM - somehow deftly eluding the scrutinizing eyes of the beach police which at one point shined their spotlights all around us. We felt like the wildest kids in the world. There were no drugs and no sex - in those days you just didn't do that kind of stuff - but we felt like a couple of really wild kids.

We spent the night sleeping on the floor at Ransome's friends' apartment. I didn't really like my date, though. She was pretty in a way that I wasn't attracted to. She had long black hair, big lips and big eyes; that can be pretty combination, but it wasn't really my style. I liked her, but not enough to try to stay near her over the summer, or to prevent me from taking a hitch-hiking trip to Panama. She probably didn't like me that much either.

By the time summer arrived after my sophomore year, I was ready for a break. I was 19 years old. I had saved up $150 and I felt as rich as I had ever been. A week after we got home from school I called Fred to see what he was doing. He had saved up $80 and didn't have a summer job yet either. During the Spring we had called the Mexican consulate and some other Central American consulates in San Diego to find out what paperwork we would need to travel south. All we needed was a tourist pass for each country and permission slips from our parents.

We located all the necessary consulates and one afternoon my father drove us around to get everything signed, notarized and ready to go. We went to the local army surplus store and each bought a three-foot deep green canvas duffle bag and a mess kit. I helped Fred find a sleeping bag; I already had one. We got a real down bag for Fred; we didn't realize it

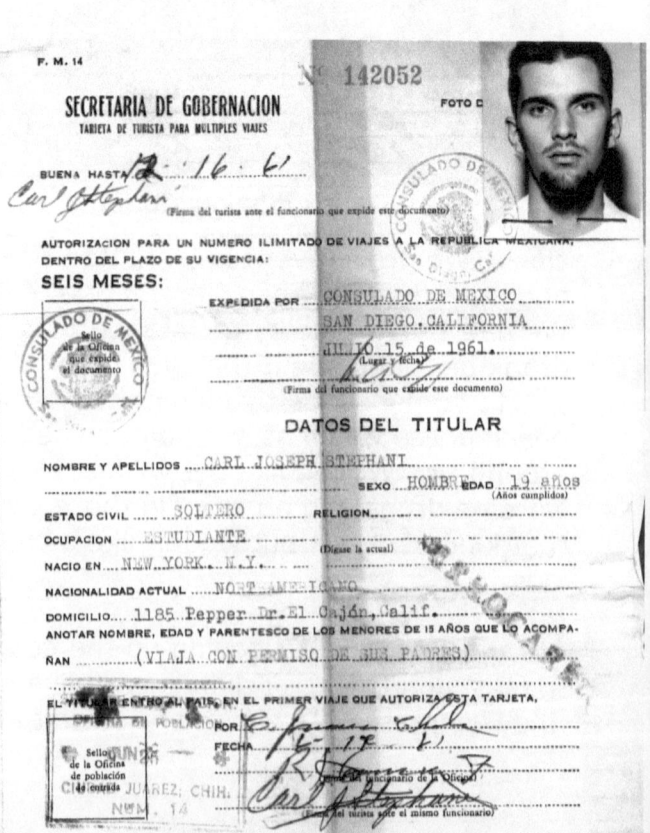

Mexico Tourist Pass

leaked feathers when we bought it, but it did leak pretty badly. Every morning when Fred would get up after sleeping in that bag he looked like a half plucked chicken - but he never got chilly.

My Mom made us some fried chicken, but until the actual day of departure I still wasn't sure we were going to do it. On the morning of Saturday, June 17, 1961, Fred came over to my place with his green canvas bag stuffed with thirty pounds of gear - sleeping bag, mess kit, change of clothes, family pictures, map, legal papers, and some other junk. I had my stuff ready too. There seemed no reason not to go.

At noon my Mom drove us to the corner of Pepper Drive and Old Route 80 in El Cajon, dropped us off, and waved goodbye.

We had tried to get Ross to join us but I think he thought we would never really do it, so he hadn't gotten ready. I couldn't believe we were actually doing it either, even when we were standing beside the two lane highway with our thumbs up in the air.

That day I wore a white, short sleeved polo shirt with a pocket, red suspenders and blue jeans. In addition to my green bag, I carried a old leather satchel, like a doctor's bag - the leather was so old and dried out that bits of it just kept crumbling off as my leg brushed against it. Fred had his green bag and the bag of food my mother had given us. He wore a long sleeved shirt and blue jeans. Fred was clean shaven. Ever since high school I had worn a mustache and goatee. Fred looked pretty much like he came out of a J. C. Penney's store with proper clothes and a good attitude. He had nice hair. We both wore hats. I had a cream colored fedora, he had a white cowboy hat. We were quite a striking looking couple of guys, *fashionistas* some would say.

We stood on the highway "thumbing" for less than half an hour when a fellow traveling to Atlanta picked us up. We drove with him for fourteen hours when he dropped us off in El Paso, Texas, at the intersection of the highway south to Ciudad Juarez, Mexico. We hiked the half mile or so south, crossed the bridge across the international border with our green bags over our shoulders, and hiked another quarter mile or so on south a bit to the train station.

Carl, Fred June 17, 1961, ready to start THE TRIP. Ross came along later.

Approximate route from San Diego to Mexico City

CHAPTER 3 - MEXICO

> "...I never really been, but I just got to go..."
> *Mexico*, James Taylor

When we got to the train station, all we wanted to do was lie down. The station itself was locked up and dark, although the railroad yard was well lighted. We walked around looking for a place to sleep, but there were no benches or anything like furniture. We also noticed that there was a night watchman at the station.

I've got an idea, Fred - let's just hop in one of these freight cars, like the guys do in the movies.

Can you just do that? I mean, are you allowed to just jump in these cars??... what if we get caught or picked up by the police or something?...

They don't care about that kind of stuff down here... there's hundreds of cars here and half of 'em are empty ... who's gonna' know ... who's gonna' care... who's gonna' do anything about it?..

Fred didn't have a good answer for that, so we headed out to the tracks to look for an open car.

As we started, we noticed out of the corners of our eyes that the night watchman, who had been sitting on the train station deck, stood up and stretched. Then he started walking along the station deck.

Hey, the watchman's getting up, Carl... I don't think we're allowed out here...,

Just keep walking like we know what we're doin'... don't look like you're interested in him... just keep walking.... watchmen .. they're like dogs... they can sense when a person is scared.. then they come after you... just keep following me...

We slipped between a couple of railroad cars thinking that would cut his view of us, but by then he must have seen that scared look in us and he kind of looked like he was making a weak effort to keep an eye on us.

He stepped down off the concrete station deck and began to shuffle kind of in our direction. Maybe he was following us, maybe he wasn't; like if he lost track of us he wouldn't really care, but if it wasn't too inconvenient, he was going to keep us in view.

We took a couple of quick steps around the end of another railroad car, thinking we could escape him by ducking under the second car. He was craftier than we had anticipated; he cut directly across the end of two cars and when we came up from beneath the car that we had ducked under, he was right at the end of it looking down at us like he was absolutely ready to pull a gun - so I said it! - "*Queremos dormir!*" - we want to sleep!

I could have just as easily said "*Queremos dormir* - so don't kill us!" - but I didn't want Fred to know how scared I was, so I left it at "We want to sleep!" That was the first mandatory Spanish I had ever spoken in my life. Once you get the first mandatory sentence behind you, the rest is a cakewalk. The hardest sentence is the first one you absolutely have to speak - and for a moment in that railroad yard, I thought my life was on the line when I spoke it. Once the first sentence is out, the rest of it is just like any other job, but you have to do it once to realize that..

"*Que buscan ...?*" What are you looking for, he asked. "*Queremos dormir, queremos viajar en el tren...mañana..*" We want to ride on the train, I responded. He recognized that we were foreigners and kindly spoke to us very slowly. Our Spanish was quite wooden, but we got across our message and he led us back to the station where he asked his boss, who had been snoozing inside, if we could sleep on the station landing.

"*Esta bien..*" -that's alright- we understood him to say.

The stranger and Carl sleeping on the train station landing, Ciudad Juarez, Mexico

There already was another guy sleeping on a wooden hand cart on the station deck, so we rolled out our sleeping bags just down the way from him to sleep the few hours until morning. It was beautiful weather for traveling.

Our bodies relaxed right into the landing like sacks of flour; our minds were another problem.

Carl..., did you see those guys go by over toward town? What do you think they are doing?

I don't know. Three other guys just walked around back of the station.. I could just see their shadows.

I don't think they'll bother us ... do you?

Hey, let's think about it... what the heck do we have that anyone in the world would want, even in Mexico...?

I don't think we have anything... but what if they're a gang... or just some wackos or something..?

Hey, we're right under this light, and none of them are going to want to do anything out here where they can be seen ... Hey, c'mon, I'm zapped, man...Let's just go to sleep.

I hear you, but like twenty guys just walked across the tracks over there where we were... what the heck can they be up to? ... this gives me the creeps....

Who knows, man... let's just keep one eye open and glance around between snoozing.. we have to get some rest... I don't think they want to get us...

As the sun's glow began to lighten the eastern sky, I whispered - Hey.. Fred, you awake..?..

Whaddya' mean, am I awake.!?.. You mean you went to sleep! ... there's been at least two hundred guys walking out there in the last few hours and they all look to me like killers... you mean you slept through all this!

Not that I know of, but, thank God, I think it's about time for the night to be over. Let's just get up... this is a stupid waste of time.. I'm more tired now than I was when we laid down....

We rolled up our sleeping bags and I brushed the feathers off Fred.

Understanding that we could get a coach-class train ticket that would take us all the way to Mexico City for a few dollars, we asked the watchman what the deal was. By this time, he seemed to be taking some personal interest in us. He explained how we could buy our train tickets and where we could buy some food *"muy barrato"* (very cheap).

We were up much too early to buy breakfast, even though there were some tourists and loads of locals on the streets already, so we just wandered for a while. We still had some fried chicken and gumdrops left from what my Mom had given us; we bought sodas and bread to go with them.

At 9 AM the Banco Provincial del Norte, S.A., opened and we went in to cash a traveler's check to get some pesos to buy our train tickets. The watchman had told us to buy our tickets early and to speak Spanish when we did because there were many people who wanted tickets, and not much room.

In line we attempted to speak Spanish to an old man who told us that his 93 year old mother had just died. He was very sad and very emotional. To make conversation with him, I asked him where could I get a stamp to mail a letter that I had just written to my mother. At that point tears came to his eyes and he insisted that I give him my letter and that he would mail it for me. He told me how lucky I was to still have a mother who was alive and said it would be a privilege for him to mail my letter for me. I told him I knew I was lucky, my Mom was the one who made the chicken for this trip.

Eight dollars and fifty cents each bought us the right to ride on wooden slats all the way to Mexico City for the next three days and two nights.

CHAPTER 4 - THE TRAIN

"Con hambre no, hay mal pan."
"When you are hungry, nothing tastes bad."
Spanish Folk Saying

The train started chugging southward with a couple hundred poor, but very friendly, Mexican people and two American college kids at about 1:30 that afternoon.

As we were lining up to get on the train, an older man, obviously a "*gringo*," approached us.

My wife will be getting off this train tomorrow with these kids and all these packages. I would sure appreciate it if you boys could help her get all this stuff off..,

Sure.., we'd be glad to help. Are they going on a vacation?

No, they're just going back home. They live in Mexico where Claudina was born; I live in Texas.

Wow! How long have you been doing that?

Ever since we got married about fifteen years ago.

Gosh! Isn't that kind of hard to do..? or do you get together quite a bit?...

Well, it is a little annoying sometimes, but we get together every six months or so and we really appreciate each other when we do... "

How did you ever meet?

I was on a military assignment in Mexico. We met one evening at a dinner, and soon after that we decided to get married... Well, thanks for the help boys... we'll be seeing you...

The train whistle blew several times and we started slowly lurching forward.

That was the last we saw of Bill, but we enjoyed spending the next day with Claudina and her sons Alfredo, Jose, Offrer, Pedro, and Juanito. Offrer was ten years old and in the middle of his brothers. He became our good buddy because he wanted to learn English. He laughed at Fred's Spanish saying "He sounds like a barking cat when he speaks Spanish." I never did understand what he meant by a barking cat, but Offrer was never nasty, so it must have meant something alright. He joked with us with a real sense of humor, and we really got to liking him.

Fred, what do you think of Bill and this family situation?

I think Bill is a cad, and I think maybe he has another family in Texas. I think Claudina is a pretty lady, but she must be half his age...

I agree. I feel kind of sorry for the family... but I guess they're doing what they can...

Shortly after sunset the train brakes suddenly started squealing, the whistle blowing, and we all found ourselves resisting sliding forward out of our seats. We were making a shorter stop than one of the normal ones we had made coming into the other small town stations.

What the heck is happening?? "*Que pasa*" we heard up and down our car.

We leaned our heads out the windows but it was much too dark to see anything but the headlight of the engine and a bit of the tracks up ahead. There were lanterns and some activity up front, so Fred, Offrer and I hopped off the train and ran up to the engine along with a multitude of other folks.

Train to Mexico City rounding a turn

"*Que pasa!*" "*Que pasa!*" was the common cry, and we soon saw what the problem was. The train in this area passed alongside a huge wash. In the dry season that was no problem, but there had recently been a rainstorm and the bank along which the railroad track passed was washed out right up to the edge of the railroad ties.

It took six hours for the repair crew to load enough rock rip-rap along the bank for them to allow us to pass, so we got to spend an extra six hours on the train on our way to Mexico City.

We had hoped not to have something like that happen because, even without delays, the three day ride on the wooden slats soon became quite painful.

Fred and Carl on the train from Ciudad Juarez to Mexico City

There are only so many different sitting positions you can assume in relation to a row of wooden slats, and before too long, you have to begin repeating positions from one sore spot on your butt to another. The benches weren't long enough for us to lie on, so the only place to lie down where you could stretch out would have been the floor. Half the lights were out on the train; the air conditioning was - as expected - by means of open windows. The smell of the lavatories pervaded all the rail cars, and it wasn't nice. We were afraid to wash our hands in the lavatories for fear of getting them dirty!

The floors of these passenger trains were another story. The trains looked like they had been in service for several hundred years and the people who used them were accustomed to spitting, carrying stuff in on their shoes, and generally not being too concerned about what landed on the floor. The chickens, goats, dogs, and other animals that rode along with their owners didn't help matters any. For that reason, for the first six hours anyway, as far as sleeping was concerned, the floor wasn't an option.

We passed through dozens of small towns most of which were very rural with mostly dirt roads. During the first part of the trip we went through very rocky mountainous terrain where there was some agriculture and everything was made of stone - fences, homes, sheds, and barns. Oxen were used to plow the fields which were also full of rocks. The doors of every home in the towns we passed through would have at least one person standing in them as the train went by, and every time we stopped, we were swarmed by people of all ages, shapes and sizes offering to sell us their home-made food and fruits.

By twelve hours into the trip we were really getting tired and, because we couldn't stretch out anywhere to get the rest we needed, we started getting giddy instead. To play around with our minds, we began to speak in German. We fastened on the word "*giftig*", which means "dirty," and we began to joke with each other about all the *giftig* things we could see on the train, laughing at each other's comments, and keeping each other awake. The Mexicans in the car seemed to want to be amused with us, but, let's face it, it was getting late, and they had no idea what we were talking about.

We went on with the *giftig* thing till the wee hours of the morning when we were nodding off in jolts of sleep sitting on the wooden benches. My mind started going *giftig* on its own. I began wondering what was dirtier, the deck of the train station we had slept on, or the floor of the railroad car. I found myself wondering how many people had spit on the train floor and balancing that against the likelihood of permanently damaging my limbs by continuing to prevent them from stretching out completely. I looked around at the chickens hanging from the coat hangars with their feet tied together, and the other animals on the train, and I wondered if the organic composition of animal waste should make it less objectionable as bedding material.

After about 14 hours on the train, at about 3 am, I found myself semi-consciously unrolling my sleeping bag on the floor beneath the slatted wooden bench upon which Fred and I had been sitting. The next thing I knew, I found myself crawling into my unrolled sleeping bag on the floor of the railroad car beneath the slatted wooden bench and totally forgetting about how anyone else might have ever used the floor of that railroad car for anything at any time in the past. Boy! It felt sooo good to stretch out...

We made good friends with Offrer and his family, even though they only spoke Spanish. Offrer helped us a lot. He showed us where the toilets were, and got us sodas when we didn't know where to get them. He really liked to laugh at our Spanish, but he was good to practice with. It was so much fun being in a situation that required speaking Spanish. Fred had never formally studied Spanish, although he had bought a Spanish textbook before we left San Diego. I had studied four different foreign languages and was able to get along somewhat well in Spanish.

Offrer's family got off at Aguas Calientes with hugs and kisses all around. They invited us to visit, and we thanked them for their friendship; then we were alone again.

The train stopped at every little town, and there was one at least every hour along the way. After a day or two Fred got off the train at one of these small towns to see about buying something to eat. He wanted to buy some "*pan*"- plain bread. As he got off, a half dozen little Mexican kids in tattered clothing came on board selling their little "*gorditos*" - like little sandwiches. At the same station, a family boarded the train and sat down on the bench across the aisle from us and began eating lunch, which consisted of several little home made "*gorditos*". They were laughing and having a great time until they noticed me across the aisle. I was sitting all alone and I must have looked pretty forlorn. In any case they must have pitied me because they offered me one of their gorditos.

"Oh, no, *gracias*..." I said, but they wouldn't take "no" for an answer; they were concerned about my welfare.

"Oh, *sí*", they insisted, and I couldn't refuse. Their young son handed me a gordito which I acknowledged with "*Gracias*".

With a big smile I finally bit into this wonderful little loaf of bread, actually happy to have some bulk to fill my empty stomach, and not really caring what was inside.

Then, just as suddenly as I had bitten into the sandwich, I felt my mouth on fire, with a torch heading for my throat! I swallowed hoping somehow it would go away, but instead of leaving my mouth, the flames just expanded to my throat.

The whole family was looking at me expectantly. I tried to speak - absolutely no voice. Absolutely nothing! I felt like I was lucky to be breathing. My throat was in flames. I just looked over at them and gave them a weak, teary-eyed smile. I think they began to realize that something was not altogether right, and, not wanting to embarrass me, they asked me if I would like a demitasse of coffee. I shook my head 'yes' and they poured some coffee from a thermos they had into a demitasse and passed it across the aisle to me.

I drank the coffee and began to feel some slight relief. The coffee itself was unlike any I had ever had, but it felt a lot better than the sandwich. It was more like a syrup than a beverage - as though they had half-filled their thermos with sugar and then poured coffee in on top of it. I really didn't like the coffee, but the hot chili pepper from the sandwich was worse, so I drank up till there were just coffee grinds in the bottom of the cup.

Just about the time my tears were drying and my throat was giving me back some of my voice, Fred boarded the train with his little loaf of plain white bread.

Hey, Carl - what are you eating?

I could barely get the words out without breaking into a very juvenile giggle. He knew that something was fishy because he knew I didn't like any kind of coffee, and he must have been wondering why I was drinking it.

Oh, this family gave me one of their sandwiches. That was really nice of them...

I looked over toward the family and nodded "yes," which was also meant as a thank you.

Would you like to try some of it?

The sandwich was on a roll about the size of a kaiser roll and I had only taken one large bite out of it.

Sure! Thanks!

Fred took a big bite out of the sandwich and went thru his ordeal by fire. They offered him some coffee too, which he also accepted, even though he didn't normally didn't drink coffee either.

We ate the rest of the bread of the sandwich, discretely avoiding the chili pepper inside it which I slipped into my pocket when I thought no one could see me do it.

When Fred had stepped off the train, he had bought two tacos for half a peso. There was some lettuce on them and we had always been told that lettuce could carry problem bacteria. He ate the tacos anyway, mostly avoiding the lettuce.

The last day on the train was no longer fun.   We began to call everything "*giftig*" and we got so giddy that all one of us would have to say is "*giftig*" and the other one would just break up laughing. We called everything "*giftig*". We looked like we were *giftig*. I looked like a scarecrow with my goatee, and Fred had grown a bit of his sparse beard and looked, if I may say, almost as scraggly.

CHAPTER 5 - MEXICO CITY

"You can observe a lot, just by watching"
- Yogi Berra

Three days after boarding, we got off the train in Mexico City at about six in the evening. The final stretch of track went through some unbelievable slums on the way to the train station, but the station itself was very nice. We stuffed all our belongings into our bags and walked out to the street to look at MEXICO CITY!

Fred at the Mexico City train station

That evening was absolutely beautiful, even a little cool. The Mexican taxi drivers seemed accustomed to the daily train arrivals as they swarmed all over everyone who had a suitcase or a bag. One unfortunate driver managed to get us into his cab; by that time we had decided to spend our first night in Mexico City in a hotel.

Not knowing anything about the place, we just asked the cabbie to take us to the nicest inexpensive hotel nearby that he knew of. He headed out one way for several minutes and pulled up to a fairly nice looking hotel; jumped out; then came back to tell us that they didn't have any rooms. Then he took us to another, then another, finally on the fifth hotel we decided we had enough of this fellow. We paid our cab fare and hiked down the street on our own.

I think the driver was either just trying run up our fare, or to get us to a hotel where he would get a cut. He would hop out of the cab in front of us at each place we stopped and run ahead of us into the hotel and give the clerk some kind of greeting. Then when we asked for a room we were told that none were available. The first hotel we went into without his help had a room for us right away, although we had to pay what we felt was an outrageous US$4 for the night!

After checking in, we spent the rest of the evening just walking around downtown Mexico City. We found Sanborn's Restaurant which was where all the "ugly Americans" ate, and we ordered a hamburger and shake. We were really ugly Americans at that point, but we had American money and that was good enough to buy a meal at Sanborn's.

Carl looking fearless on a Mexico City sidewalk

We got lost walking around the city and spent a good two hours walking in a six block area from the hotel to the central post office and then trying to find our way back. It was a cool, beautiful summer evening and we had no need to rush. That night at the hotel, we propped a canteen upside down against the door in case anyone were to try to break in; we clutched our money and stuck our hands in our pillow cases; and had our pocket knives open at our bedsides. This was the first hotel either of us had ever stayed in alone, so we thought that was what you did.

Fred was very cautious. He would not drink any water, anywhere, without putting a water purifying tablet in it. He put tablets in the water they gave us at Sanborn's! Sanborn's was like the McDonalds of Mexico City. I was embarrassed; but, to his credit, at least he survived the whole trip without ever getting "the runs". Maybe the pills weren't such a bad idea! Anyway, he got over the pill thing eventually further down in Mexico.

The next day, June 21, 1961, we took a bus out to the University. It was pouring rain. The buildings there were like a gigantic collection of artworks. We were stunned by the beauty of it all. Our university looked like a warehouse in comparison. We talked with one of the students who was washing dishes there and got the impression that he really appreciated the place and was quite proud of it. The students were all dressed up, like at some Eastern university in the United States.

In the evening we walked out to the stadium which was supposed to hold 100,000 people. All the gates were locked, so we climbed over a chain-link fence to get inside. We walked around the stadium a little and then settled down underneath some seats near the centerline of the field, a few rows up from the turf. We unrolled our sleeping bags on the concrete floor beneath the stands and crawled in and tried to fall asleep. Sometime around midnight we heard the stadium gates being opened; chains rattling. We heard talking and dogs, and in the moonlight, as we peeked over the backs of the stadium seats, we saw two watchmen walking along the running track.

"What should we do?" Fred asked in as tiny a whisper as he could muster. "Should we stand up and turn ourselves in.... what if they see us and shoot us before we can explain who we are... what if we don't turn ourselves in and the dogs sniff us out!?!.... "

Shhh.... Shhhh....

We lay back down. They walked within fifty feet of us. We lay still and quiet. They stopped, chatted for a while, and then continued on, dogs and all. We made it! Victory!! Sleep at last, sleep at last, good God Almighty, we could sleep at last!

Through the night various people came into the stadium, including one romantic couple that came very close to discovering us, but we remained hidden all night.

The next day we went back downtown, tired and hungry. Our first stop was the central post office where we checked for mail at General Delivery - we both had mail!! I had a note from my Mom, and Fred had a note from his girlfriend, Sally. Sally told us that Ross had left for Mexico City and she gave us the address of some people in their church that he would stay with when he arrived.

We ordered pancakes at Sanborn's that morning and planned to head south the following day. Before we left Mexico City we wanted to visit some of the consulates. They all closed at 2 pm, so we had to hustle. It seemed like we were constantly worried about having all the proper paper work we needed; but, as it turned out, we always had more papers than we ever needed.

As we walked through downtown Mexico City, hungry, tired, and lonely we had no idea where we were going to sleep that night, and I was developing a pretty severe case of the "runs" - needing to run to the bathroom all the time. We were beginning to wonder why we had set out on this trip, and whether we should just turn around and go back to the comfortable beds, warm showers, and abundant food that was waiting for us at home.

Slouching forward with our bags over our shoulders at midday, we walked through the crowds along the sidewalk bordering the Bosque de Chapultepec, Mexico City's huge central park, not really knowing what we were going to do next, until in that city of nearly five million the unimaginable happened!!

John!!! Ransome!!! You guys decided to make the trip!! You look like a couple of American playboys! Boy! Are you a sight for sore eyes!! When did you get down here? What are you doing?

Ah, we're just walking around. I ran across some people I know from LA who live here now, and they gave us the keys to a three-bedroom place they own that's vacant this month. We're going to look around here for a while, and then head down to my folks' place in British Honduras.

Ransome's friends' house in Mexico City

What are you guys doing?

We have absolutely no idea. We spent last night sleeping under the bleachers at the University stadium. We have no idea what we're doing ...

Hey, come stay with us! The place is huge, and it's empty! There's plenty of room for you two, and it's not far from here. You can shower, change, and we can get something cheap for dinner. There are all kinds of places around here.

You got it, man! We're with you! What a godsend you two are! We're with you! Wow! We love you guys!!! We're your friends for life!!!

The next day my diarrhea got really terrible, so I was out of commission for a while. Fortunately, we were able to eat some good meals and sleep comfortably for a couple of days to get ready for the rest of the trip.

The day before we were to leave we took a bus out to the pyramids. They were really impressive - gigantic with miles and miles of partly yet uncovered ruins of the ancient city. We saw stadia, little villages of houses, and all sorts of different buildings. It was an all day trip from Mexico City but it was well worth the fifty cents it cost to get there.

That evening we got a city street map and found our way on a series of dirt roads to the address Sally had given us to find Ross.

We knocked on the door at about eight o'clock and a little old Mexican lady peeked through a window at us. We tried to explain who we were, when suddenly the door flew open and there he was - looking just like he had stepped off the stage - he always dressed well and looked so neat!

Somehow it was great to see him again, and we gave each other great big *abrazos*, hugs. The family fed us a little dinner, and we left with Ross for Ransome's place. Ross was so unflappable; it was great to have him with us.

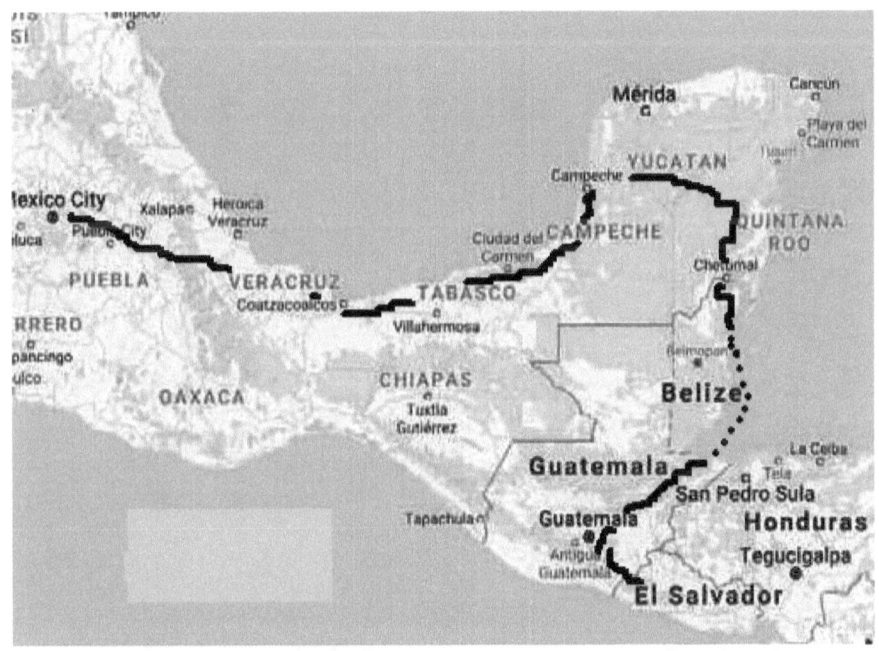
Approximate route from Mexico City to El Salvador
Map data ©2018 Google, INEGI

CHAPTER 6 - VERA CRUZ AND THE YUCATAN

> "Let everyone sweep in front of his own door
> and the whole world will be clean"
> Johann Wolfgang von Goethe

The five of us left Mexico City on a Saturday night train for Vera Cruz on the Gulf of Mexico. The trains were very inexpensive and in the heavily urbanized areas we felt that our money would be better spent on them than on the meals it would take to feed us if we took several days to hitchhike the same distance. About half way to Vera Cruz we stopped in a little town where we had to change trains. Our connecting train was late and we had to wait thirty six hours for a connecting train to come through.

The whole length of the train ride from Mexico City was stunning. The railroad tracks were cut through dense green jungle, and in the distance you could see the snow-covered peaks of the mountains to the south. The contrast was so dramatic - to look at jungle birds and animals and a wild jungle river out one window, and then catch glimpses of snow covered Mount Orizaba off in the distance out another. Not having seen anything like this in our lives, we were enthralled by the beauty of the scenery.

The train to Vera Cruz was much cleaner than the train from Ciudad Juarez, and was a pleasure to ride. By this time we had gotten more used to eating local foods and when the train stopped at little towns along the way, and the women and children came aboard with their big pots full of fresh, home cooked hot meals, we began to get into the swing of buying from them.

Along this stretch of railway a little eight year old kid who had a pot full of little "*gorditos*" that looked like little fat pancakes came on board. I bought a couple of his gorditos and "Wow!" were they delicious! I would have bought a dozen, but before I tasted how good they were, the train had been cleared and the kid with the pot was gone.

Those little things were like sourdough pancakes with the maple syrup cooked right into them. They were chewy and just plain delicious. I could have eaten fifty. I never saw anything just like them again. I asked a lot of cooks about them and the only answer I ever got was that they must have been some local version of a *gordito*.

The town where we had our layover was built on several hills in the middle of the jungle. We walked up and down the hills to get whatever views of the area we could. The views in town were of greenery and more greenery contrasted against the white clay caliche of the dirt roads.

Town on the way from Mexico City to Vera Cruz - view from the train "station"

We bought tacos from a street vendor and a couple of us drank a bottle of beer with our tacos. We felt like we were finally really getting away from the United States. Here we were in a little town, with dirt streets cut out of the jungle where all you could hear were the sounds of the wildlife and an occasional little noise from someone's radio.

The biggest thing to happen in town was the arrival of the train every several days. Nothing to do but talk with people and hang out. It seemed like the land where time stood still and we were really ready for that kind of experience. No way to rush anything, no hustle, no bustle, - just jungle and a few people huddled together around their modest little houses with the occasional chug of a railroad train.

Kids played with hoops in the streets, rolling them with sticks; men played dominoes. Somebody must have been working somewhere, but aside from the merchants and railroad personnel, it wasn't obvious who was working where. We five *gringos* fit right in, strange as that may seem, because we were in no hurry either - we just enjoyed a good (half understood) conversation with the locals; and the locals were magnificently friendly. We spent a nice day and a half there and slept on the ground by the train station.

Even there, however, it seemed like I was always overwhelmingly tired from not sleeping well. I bought an extra shirt and a snorkel in town, and a diving mask that I hoped to be able to use when we got to the coast the next day. I love to swim and I was really looking forward to getting to the coast again. In addition, the inland towns always seemed poorer than the coastal towns.

We didn't stay in Vera Cruz more than a few hours before our next train left for Coatzacoalcos. Vera Cruz was very hot, but also very scenic. Most of the stores near the waterfront had wooden porches and sidewalks, and it was easy there to imagine oneself in a western movie with a lot of Mexican people around. I would have liked to have stayed a while longer in Vera Cruz, but the others over-ruled me and we cut our stay short.

We arrived in Coatzacoalcos at night and asked a somewhat inebriated bystander where we could rent a cheap hotel room. He led us around the city until we finally found a place for about forty cents each for the night. They wouldn't let us see the room before we rented it, but it was raining and we needed a place to stay, so we took it. The lights were out in most of the city because of the storm - it was June 27th - but we just wanted a place to sleep.

Carl, Ransome and others in our "hotel" room in Coatzacoalcos, Mexico

We laughed our heads off when we saw the room, all five of us. What a HOLE! It was on the second floor; the first floor was just four exterior walls with a bathroom to the side. Our room was about twelve feet square with two absolutely ancient double beds in it and two incredibly old beat up mattresses. There was also a bucket of water in the room which we didn't know whether we could drink so we used it for washing up.

A tremendous downpour started shortly after we got in the room with lightening striking all around the town. Since we were all pretty dirty and smelly at that point, we took off our shirts, went out on the balcony, and let the rain pour down on us. Then Ransome wanted to take a regular shower, so he and Ross went down to the first floor where there was a shower stall of sorts. Just before they were to get in the shower, another hotel guest walked by them and got in. Then a sharp clap of lightening hit across the street and they all abandoned the shower idea for a while.

Ransome had a tin of camp stove fuel which he lit up to have some light in the room. The room looked like an explosion had occurred in a Salvation Army collection center - shoes and clothing strewn all over the place!

After a while the lights came on in town again. Ross and Ransome went out to look over the town. They put on their rain coats and Ross grabbed his big hunting knife. Their walk around town was uneventful.

We got up the next morning and caught a city bus down to the beach to spend the day. We had two snorkels and two diving masks and went swimming around the hull of a ship that had foundered there years ago. The beach was composed of beautiful white sand, and the water was wonderfully warm!

Ross caught a two pound super ugly fish with his bare hands, and a local fisherman with a spear gun and a dozen fish on a string on the shore shouted "*cuidado!*" when he saw it because apparently the spines on the fish were poisonous.

In the afternoon we tried some spear fishing. I had found an old broom handle which we lashed to Ross' hunting knife. We never succeeded in spearing one thing so we bought 15 fish from the guy with the real spear gun.

Fred got tangled up in some fishing line when he went swimming, and he pulled in the line, which had a hook on it. He used the line and a piece of the fish Ross had caught to catch a little half pound fish for us. Ross walked into town a couple of blocks and found a place to buy some oil, onions, salt and pepper and we made a little fire among the rocks that jutted out into the water by the carcass of the old ship and had a great little fish cookout on the beach! It was a great day, even though we all got a little sunburned.

That night we went to the bus station and waited for about three hours for a bus to Campeche, which would be about half way toward Merida on the Yucatan Peninsula. When it finally arrived at midnight we got into it and sat down on its unimaginably bouncy seats. You couldn't sit on the seats, you just kind of sat on top of them as though you were sitting on a plastic bag full of jello.

When the bus started moving we started rolling around. We rolled uncontrollably into each other all night as the bus stopped and started, turned and braked. We rolled along and struggled to keep ourselves from laughing out loud for the whole night and half of the next day when we arrived at Campeche - exhausted again but ready to laugh at the drop of a hat because of the funny seat experience.

On the way to Campeche, the bus had to stop every so often to be ferried across one of the many rivers that flow into the Gulf. At one stop when the bus had to wait for a ferry, we picked up some coconuts that had fallen to the ground and a local fellow offered to whack off the tops for us with his machete so we could get at the milk and meat. They were great, and you couldn't complain about the cost!

A Jamaican fellow in a nice American car was keeping pace with our bus on the roadway and each time we stopped Ransome would go talk with him. He was driving from Los Angeles to Corozal, the first town in British Honduras after you cross the border from Chetumal in Mexico, and he had room for a couple of people in his car. After half a dozen or so stops, Ransome had befriended the guy and he offered Ransome a ride. Ransome took John and they both left us to ride with the Jamaican. I must admit that I envied them. The bus was actually painful to ride in.

Ross, Fred and I continued in the bus until we got to Campeche. We didn't want to stay in Campeche long because we were getting anxious to get to Ransome's place with its more familiar food and culture. So, after getting off the "tour" bus, we boarded a municipal bus and took it as far out of the City as possible in an easterly direction, toward the inland city of Peto. At the end of the bus route we continued walking a mile or so to get away from the urbanized area until we were pretty much all alone alongside the highway.

We waited for an hour or so, trying to flag down one of the vehicles that occasionally drove by until, finally, the driver of a flatbed truck stopped to pick us up. The truck was carrying wood split for shake shingles piled about 15 foot high and tied down with ropes. (Picture a man with an extraordinarily bloated belly lying on his back and put wheels on him and you have the silhouette made by this truck).

We were invited to climb up on top of the shingles to ride with a wild Cuban guy who had also hitched a ride. The Cuban told us jokes and laughed the entire way, even though he must have noticed that we couldn't understand half of what he was saying what with the 50 mph wind and his heavy accent. Cubans run all their words together and this guy was a pure Cuban with no concern for how slowly us three "*gringos*" were able to think in Spanish.

At the same time as the Cuban was regaling us with his incomprehensible stories, we were trying to hold on for dear life as the truck veered and swung along the dirt roads that would take us toward Peto. We rode like that for about an hour. The Cuban guy was somewhat of an acrobat as well as a comedian because he stayed on the truck effortlessly - he just leaned and rolled as the truck lurched, swung, bounced and turned, as though he had been glued to the shingles at his hips.

The ride got even more exciting after about an hour when it started pouring rain. Ross and Fred, who were riding in the middle of the load, started trying to get their ponchos out. I was sitting on the front with my feet on the roof of the cab twisted around looking back at them. On one turn, Fred almost slid off the woodpile but Ross grabbed him, pulled him back and they finally got out their ponchos.

After half an hour or so of rain, we stopped in a little town for the drivers to get something to eat. We bought a couple of tamales for ourselves while we were waiting when a middle-aged Mexican salesman from Proctor & Gamble pulled up and asked us where we were going. We told him we were headed for Belize and since he was heading in the same direction, he offered us a ride.

Just then the truck drivers came back with a couple of big papayas they had bought for us. They thought we were impoverished so we accepted them but told them we were going with the other guy because he had a car and we could ride inside. We tried to thank them for their ride and the kindness of the papayas, but they wouldn't accept our thanks. They were very, very humble, very kind guys.

We noticed that in the Yucatan the people really seemed to consider the word "*gracias*" (thanks) as a gift. They didn't just casually say "Thanks".   When someone said "*gracias*" to them they treated it like something material they were receiving and, if they didn't think they deserved it, they just wouldn't accept it. They would say "*no*" when you offer your thanks and would sometimes insist that the thing they had done for you was really not enough to be thanked for. Because in high school we all seemed to elevate sarcasm to the highest level of art, we were often surprised to meet and deal with so many apparently guileless people who didn't carry sarcasm around constantly in their hearts - it was quite a contrast and a great pleasure for us.

We rode with the Proctor and Gamble salesman in his little Hillman for about 2 hours until we arrived at the town of Muna. Before he headed north to Merida he invited us to visit his home some day and offered to give us a first class sightseeing tour of the city. He also showed us to the local "*Presidencia*" in Muna. The *Presidencia* was a place where we could sleep, have our "luggage" guarded, and use a very clean bathroom for free. He told us that many Mexican villages have a "*Presidencia*" and we got the impression that a *Presidencia* is where the mayor's office was and also where the jail and the town police were located.

We spent the night in the Muna town *Presidencia*. In the morning when Ross got up he went out the east door where he was greeted by a policeman who asked him for 20 *pesos* each from us for a boarding fee. Ross told the policeman that he would be back after he spoke with me and Fred.

Fred and I were adamantly against paying because we had been told the night before by the man who dropped us off that sleeping in the *Presidencia* was free. We left by way of another door which opened onto the street and in a stroke of good fortune in a matter of minutes were riding on a beer truck to Peto! It's not that we were scofflaws, but that we felt like that policeman was just trying to scam us out of 20 pesos each.

The beer truck stopped at every little village along the way and at each place we helped the drivers unload and load their boxes of beer bottles. Riding on the beer truck was almost as exciting as riding on the wood truck because the beer cases were stacked evenly about twelve feet high and we rode on top of them.

CHAPTER 7 - PETO AND THE YUCATECAS

"Talk doesn't cook rice."
Chinese Proverb

When we got to Peto, we went to a lovely little restaurant on the town square and each bought a "*bistek*" and a soda for about US$.40. Peto was a very small town and after we had our steaks, we walked to the outskirts of town to the main road heading south to Chetumal and Corozal. We began our wait at about 10:30 in the morning sitting in the shade of the side wall of a little *tienda* (grocery store) at the edge of the town. The edge of town was pretty abrupt and right beyond this store began the miles of jungle between Peto and the next town further south.

We had no idea how much traffic traveled south from Peto and finally about noon, we began asking people if many trucks went through going to Chetumal. As well as we could understand, we were told "Oh yes..., many go by..., we get a lot of trucks in our town and every day..., five trucks carrying asbestos pipes go through headed for Chetumal, but they don't go by until about 4:00 in the afternoon. "If nothing else comes along," we were told, "you can surely get a ride with one of the *camiones con tubos*'" (pipe trucks).

The temperature stays very hot in Southern Mexico until about 6:00 it the evening. At about three in the afternoon, the owner of the store brought us each a coke, a french roll and a can of sardines. We made sardine sandwiches and had a very nice meal. He told us that he didn't think the trucks with the pipes would be coming through until about 5:00 that evening.   We told him that was "*no problema*", we could wait another hour or so easily enough.

At about five that evening a somewhat inebriated old man, who did not appear to be one of the town fathers, came by to talk with us and convinced us to go wait at the *Presidencia*. We were very leery of this old guy and his friends, but nothing much was happening on the roadway, so we went with him. He was super talkative and extremely proud of the fact that he was a Yucataca, not just a Mexican. To us he was just a scary old drunk, but to him being a Yucateca really meant something. We didn't appreciate that concept at the time, but we learned more about it.

Fred on the corner in Peto, Mexico, waiting for a ride

In the public square in the center of town we met the nicest group of people we had yet met on the trip. One young man in his twenties in particular took us into his confidence. Along with others, he assured us that by eight that evening, at the latest, the pipe trucks would be coming through. "Five of them had come through the night before."

He told us that the people of the Yucatan have a high sense of state consciousness because of the pride they have in their ancestry. They are different from other Mexicans, and like to let everyone know that by introducing themselves as Yucatecas, rather than as Mexicans. They generally called themselves by their own names followed by the word "Yucateca": For instance, *"Me llamo Jose Gutierrez, Yucateca."*

Yucatan was an especially beautiful place. Everyone in Peto wore white and the houses were all whitewashed and everything really did look clean, neat and well kept. We began to notice a difference in these people. I told the young fellow that we were afraid of getting involved in a drunken fight because quite of few of the young guys around town were getting drunk and we weren't used to so much drinking and jostling around. He assured us that they never have more than "slapstick" fights, and that they never, ever bothered outsiders. I asked him about the water in town and he assured us it was good to drink, so, for the first time in two weeks, we drank gallons of water without purification and we even ate the ice cubes.

We got so confident in the Yucatecas that we even bought some milkshakes (*horchata*) from a local vendor pushing a cart around the town square. These milkshakes were different from American milkshakes. They consisted of water with milk, and a concentrated flavor syrup over finely minced ice. I think they also added powdered rice, or almonds or coconut or some of each to the mixture which they blended up in a little household blender. They tasted delicious, and we each had a couple of big glasses of the stuff.

Fred, Ross, and I certainly were the celebrities of the night that evening in Peto. By eight in the evening the square was full of people of all ages. The children in particular seemed to be interested in the three of us. We would tell them about where we came from and how we got there in our broken Spanish, and they would hang on our words as though they were the most important things they had ever heard. After about 9:00 p.m. we began getting concerned about ever being able to leave Peto.

We continued to ask about the pipe trucks and got as many different stories as people we asked. Some said that 4 trucks went through at 5:00 p.m. and we must have missed them; some said that the day before 25 trucks went through and probably no more would go through for a couple of days; some said they would all come through at midnight; and some said they just came through from time to time.

Three University of Michigan graduate students, with plenty of room in their car, drove by and stopped to chat. They were going to Corozal, but they did not want anyone riding with them. We never learned anything more about them and they drove off without us.

We didn't mind sleeping on the concrete steps of the Presidencia that night too much, but it was the time we felt we were losing that disturbed us, because by now we were kind of counting on getting to Panama. We began to feel that the people in town were so anxious to please us that they were telling us whatever they thought we wanted to hear rather than what they knew for certain. In any case, we spent the whole night and the next morning in Peto.

We got up quite early. Shortly after the stores opened two guys selling fish drove into town. They didn't seem very anxious to give us a ride because they didn't appear to understand the concept of hitchhiking. We talked with them for a while and finally they agreed to let us hop a ride. We climbed up on the open truck bed and began bouncing across the bumpiest dirt road through the hottest jungle that could every be imagined. Just like the other truck drivers we had ridden with, these guys also stopped at every little group of thatch roof huts or clearing in the jungle along the way. Sometimes they would stop at a small break in the jungle where a trail came through. They would wait a few minutes and, sure enough, someone would come walking out of the jungle and they would sell them some fish.

At each stop they would weigh out their orders and roll up their fish or shrimp in newspaper. Sometimes they exchanged money for their product; sometimes the exchange was in kind.

We rode with the fish mongers until about two in the afternoon when they told us they were going to stay overnight in one of the little jungle villages off of the main road. We didn't really want to spend another night in a little off-the-main-road village, so they dropped us off at a little dirt road intersection in the middle of the jungle where we almost comically began "thumbing" again on the main roadway to the south.

There was a lot of waiting to do at that intersection. Nobody drove by for hours until some time after six that evening when a truck carrying a load of bags of concrete drove by. We pleaded with them with our body language and, when we finally got them to stop, they offered us a ride to Chetumal for $.65 each. We accepted their offer and hopped on. In a couple of minutes we all looked like ghosts - covered with cement dust.

It was useless to try to resist getting covered with cement dust, so we just lay down and tried to sleep draped over the white cement bags. There was a big turkey in the truck with us that kept fluttering up every once in a while, and in addition to the $.65 each, we had the job of pushing the turkey down between the bags of cement so that he wouldn't blow off the truck. It was kind of a rough ride but not nearly as rough as the fish truck because this truck was so weighted down with concrete.

At one point, when they stopped for a "potty break," Fred

hopped off the truck to stretch his legs. The drivers apparently wanted to have some fun with him so they jumped into the truck, started it up, and abruptly gave it the gas! Fred saw the truck starting off and came running! He grabbed the sideboards at the back and tried to pull himself aboard, but couldn't quite make it and had to keep running - until, the driver hit the brakes and Fred came flying on-board! He didn't think that was very funny, but the driver sure seemed to.

We got to Chetumal, at the British Honduras border, at about one in the morning and slept again on concrete park benches in front of the Presidencia. The next morning was classic Mexico to me. At sunrise, as we sat up half out of our sleeping bags on the benches around the little central park of Chetumal, we were awakened by the sound of the drums and brass of a Mexican Army band coming out to post the colors and practice their music. They were mostly on key and just sounded like they were having a great time of it. We were their only audience and they seemed to be glad to have us there. It was a classic, beautiful sunny Mexican morning never to be forgotten.

When the band practice was over we rolled up our bags and stopped at a local restaurant for some scrambled eggs, then caught a bus down across the border to Corozal where Ransome's folks were living.

CHAPTER 8 - BRITISH HONDURAS (BELIZE)

"In youth and beauty, wisdom is rare."
Homer

We arrived in Corozal at about two in the afternoon and easily found the Wyman's two-story missionary headquarters. We were given a wonderfully warm welcome and invited to wash our clothes and take showers, which we gratefully did. As soon as we were settled in, Ransome and John invited us to go with them to one of the local beaches on a trip they had already planned. We piled into Ransome's parents' sedan and drove half a dozen miles off to the beach through the "puma-infested" jungle. They told us how a puma had grabbed a hiker walking along that road just weeks earlier. We respected the jungle even a little more after that.

As we drove along in our minds we were envisioning the beautiful beaches of Mexico and thinking of a lovely afternoon swimming and lying in the sun relaxing. What a surprise when we arrived at the "beach". It was simply the end of the road where it dipped into the ocean with no particular beauty or grace. The road was surrounded by jungle, the ocean was full of mangroves. Ransome had the key to a lock that chained up an old log dugout canoe that was attached to the trunk of one of the mangroves. We unlocked the canoe and launched it with each of us clambering aboard from the muddy tidal bottom. It was a cruddy "beach", if it could be called that at all.

Some locals were swimming there and they told us that a person six feet tall could walk for six miles out into the ocean because the river keeps bringing dirt off the land and depositing it there in a shallow alluvial fan. The beaches all along this area of the coast were all mud with rock outcrops. It was nice to be able to get cleaned up and rest with Ransome's folks and all, but the beaches of British Honduras that we saw on our trip weren't anything to write home about.

That afternoon I was asked by a couple of the locals who had checked our baggage at customs the day before to help get a fellow American from West Virginia out of jail because I could speak some Spanish. We went back across the border into Mexico to help this fellow out and everything went very well. Fred and Ross spent the day swimming and washing clothes.

On our third day in Corozal we began planning a trip to one of the off-shore "keys". We were going to stay on one of the keys for a day or two and then continue southward toward Panama, but before I got ready to go out to the islands, Fred and Ross suddenly decided to leave by hitchhiking to Belize. They were anxious to get moving south.

I wanted to see the islands, so I didn't go with them, and Ransome's folks had to drive to Belize the day after Fred and Ross left anyway in order to get their weekly mail. I thought I might catch up with them then, if I wanted to.

The next day Ransome, John and I drove with Ransome's parents leaving Corozal at about 9 AM. We drove into Belize at about 4:00 PM just as Fred and Ross were about to leave for an island key to go for a swim. We talked for a few minutes about the rest of the trip and they told me that the easiest way to get south to Guatemala from Belize would be by plane because there were no roads, and the boats were expensive. They had already bought their tickets and they convinced me to go with them.

I excused myself from the Wymans by letting them know I was going to fly out of Belize with Ross and Fred. That day, Sunday, July 2, 1961, we learned that Ernest Hemingway had shot himself, and we were all a little depressed, so we thought the beach would lighten us up. One of the mission home custodians offered to get us a boat to get out to the keys and we invited him to go along with us.

We set out in the canoe and, as soon as we found a fairly clear spot of water, we all jumped in for a swim. Soon, four black guys came paddling over to our area in their canoe. They scared us a little at first because we didn't know what they were up to. They were kind of half carelessly splashing our clothes and our boat. After a while they seemed to notice us and they initiated some conversation. As it turned out, they were just out having some fun and the area we had selected was one of the few areas where the water was clear enough to make it seem like a good place to swim.

After an hour or so, the other guys left, and we swam for another half hour and went to look at one of the picturesque little islands. It turned out to be a totally stenchy mangrove slop island, so we didn't stay. On the way back, our guide got his pole stuck in the mud and got pulled right off the boat. After he climbed back on, Ross began moving around the boat a little bit and dumped the him off again. It was pretty difficult to keep those round dugouts level. After messing around on the boat like he did, on top of a few other incidents, we began calling Ross "The Wrecker".

That evening, after we took showers, got cleaned up, and ate a good meal at the mission home, we decided to just wander around town. As we walked along the main street in a crowd of people, Fred and Ross were passed by two cute black girls. One of the girls casually patted Fred's back as she walked by, so Fred and Ross started walking to catch up with her because they thought they were going to be friendly. I was looking at some shoes in a store at the time and when I came out, I saw them standing in the middle of the street alone about 2 blocks down. When I got down to them, they told me that these two girls had walked into a group of boys standing on the corner and they were scared to go any further afraid that maybe they had caused some kind of social problem by trying to catch up with the girls.

Since I hadn't been part of the event, I just walked over and went right through the group of guys and further on to look for the girls. Fred and Ross followed. After we had passed through the group, one of the guys called out to us and started following Ross. Ross turned around and started talking to him and we thought that maybe there was a fight in the works. Fred turned around too, and then I turned because I didn't really want to walk off and leave them with a mess. As it turned out though, the guy that started talking was just a nice sociable guy looking to talk with some Americans. He told us we could have all the women we wanted for a pint of beer because their women love Americans; we were too naive and moral, to be interested.

We talked with them a while longer and I told the lead guy that I wanted to sell my heavy boots and buy a pair of lighter shoes. He asked me how much I wanted for them and I told him about 3 bucks. He told me to come visit him at the survey office where he worked the next morning because he was sure I could sell them there. Not much else happened that night and we went back to the Belize mission home and spent some time with the Beale's who were in charge there.

We slept that night on the second story veranda that surrounded the mission home. At about 2:00 in the morning a torrential rain began. All five of us grabbed up our stuff and flopped it down inside in the living room. The next morning we went down to eat breakfast with the Beales and after grace and a prayer and some other things, we finally got to eat. It was a good breakfast with butter and jelly and bread and hot cereal all the milk we wanted. We didn't dare drink milk at all on this trip, except in the houses of people we knew, because we had been warned that there might be diseases in the milk because of the way it is handled in Latin America.

After breakfast, I went over and bought my plane ticket. I sold my shoes right on the spot at the survey office and walked around town barefoot for while until I finally found a pair of nice canvas shoes, size 13 for about US$.75; which was more than I had gotten for my boots. Nevertheless, I bought them and they served me well for the rest of the trip.

After Ross got his Guatemala Visa, we went back to the Beales' and waited a few minutes for Mr. Beale to take us to the airport. First he had to take his wife to the hospital for some thing he wouldn't tell us about; then he took us to the airport where he was going to drop us off and meet his father who was arriving from the States.

We said our good-byes to John and Ransome, and made the trip from Belize to Puerto Barrios, Guatemala, by air. It only cost a dollar and fifty cents more to fly than to go by boat, and instead of 18 hours, it only took an hour and a half. I had never ridden in an airplane before. Our route was flown by a type of cargo plane with fairly crude metal seats bolted to the floor. The interior was all bare metal so that you could see every structural element of the interior of the aircraft. It made a tremendous noise, but it was an incredible thrill to look out the window and see the ground below. Another American and two women from British Honduras were on the plane with us.

CHAPTER 9 - GUATEMALA

> "The secret of being miserable is to have the leisure to bother about whether you are happy or not."
>
> George Bernard Shaw

On July 5, 1961, we arrived in Puerto Barrios and hiked a mile to the bus stop where we waited for about an hour for a bus to Guatemala City. The bus fare was three dollars, which seemed a lot to us. There was only one bus company on that route, so we had no choice there.

The converted US school bus we rode in arrived in Guatemala City at about 10:00 PM. For most of the trip, we were riding with only one other passenger, and we were the only ones who went to the end of the driver's route.

For the first time since we had left the US, we were in mountainous country with pine and palm-covered mountains all over, and big rivers. I kept watching the scenery from the time of our departure till it was dark. It was very wild looking country.

During the trip the bus driver got to know us a little. Ross established such good rapport with him that at the end of the ride he offered to let us spend the night in the bus. Before we got to sleep, half a dozen locals got on the bus to talk with us. One of them was the guy who had driven that very bus from the United States when it was first purchased by the Guatemalan bus company. He spent a bit of time telling the others how wealthy people in the United States were and we thought something problematic might be going on in their minds, but they eventually left and we stretched out on the bench seats and closed our eyes.

We slept better that night than we had slept in many a night. The next morning, the bus driver offered to take us downtown where we found the American embassy, and got a map and some other information about the area.

Before we could enter the next country on our itinerary, El Salvador, we had to get visas from the local consulate, so we spent two hours first thing in the morning searching for the Consulate. The consulate had recently moved, but when we finally found it, we were given our visas quicker than at any others - stamp, stamp, stamp and it was all done.

We spent the rest of the morning and part of the afternoon searching the streets for other consulates. We continually asked for directions, but everyone seemed to give us contradictory directions. At one point when we were way over on the east side of town, after we had started from downtown, someone told us it was way over on the west side. We gave up trying to get any other visas in Guatemala City and just starting looking for the Pan American Highway to head on to El Salvador.

We got to the highway fairly easily after wasting two hours with a guy who was sure he could get us a ride, but who never turned up with anything, so we left him. Our first hitchhiking ride in Guatemala was with an attorney who was on his way to a place near the Highway - we were about 50 miles east of the Highway at that point.

The attorney took us to within a couple of miles of the Pan American highway where he dropped us of to hike the rest of the way. The driver of the very first vehicle to go by stopped for us. Two guys were in the truck and one of them was trying to learn English so we communicated very well. They bought us three pineapples - really good ones - and told us we had several more miles to go to get to the highway.

They dropped us off at a little town on what they thought was a main highway at a place where we could wait out the rain. While we waited we could hear the noise of truck traffic, but it was coming from much further to the west. Finally, one of the guys in the town told us that the road in the town was just a cutoff road that carried local traffic.

As soon as the rain let up, we hiked about half a mile further with our bags and got to the Pan American Highway - a two-lane dirt road.

We waited there for an hour when it began to get dark and rain a little again. We were about to give up and unroll our bags in the jungle off the highway when a truck driver stopped to offer us a ride back to town so we could find a place to stay overnight.

As we approached the town, we saw a little construction worker shack, and we asked if we could stay there. The workers there took some interest in us, and said they didn't care whether we slept there or not. They also offered to show us around their construction site. They showed us how they built their scaffolding and did their construction work - a lot of rope and intricate bamboo scaffolding.

While Fred and I were looking around the place, Ross, who was waiting by the side of the highway, flagged down another truck heading south. Just when Fred and I had seen everything at the construction shack and established good rapport with the workers there, Ross came running back to tell us that he had a truck waiting to take us on south.

This truck was loaded with a few cement bags, some pipes and an old Mexican construction worker. We rode with them for about an hour until we all stopped to eat. They got a little upset with us when we didn't want to eat chicken tacos with them (for $.40 each) and even more angry when we went next door to buy some sardines and bread from a grocery store. When they came out of the café, they wanted to charge us $1.00 each for the remainder of the ride to the El Salvador border. Luckily, a black guy from Jamaica overheard our conversation and offered to give us a ride almost all the way for nothing. We accepted his offer and rode for a while in his station wagon.

As it turned out, this fellow was taking a friend of his home to a little town near the El Salvador border. His friend offered to let us sleep at his house and assured us that we could easily catch a ride from there the next morning. Everything looked rosy until we got a flat tire. There was no spare. We pulled off the wheel, but there was nothing we could do but look at it. There was a big hole in the tire and the tube.

The driver said that we might as well sleep there. He offered to catch the next truck into town to try to get another tube and tire. I went to sleep immediately and I guess he did get a ride because the next thing I knew, Fred and I were shoving our bags out of the station wagon in a deep sleep in answer to Ross' call. Ross had been waiting outside and had hailed down another vehicle. We rolled out of the wagon somehow and hopped on top of a big flatbed truck filled with some kind of gravel. These guys were going to some place near San Salvador.

Fred and I rode in the cab in order to be sociable, and these guys were very nice. They slowed down their Spanish for us and were interested in our trip. When we reached the border, they fixed up a tarp on the gravel where all five of us slept very comfortably. The next morning, I woke up early and had to scavenge a place to go to the bathroom between the walls of a new building which looked like some kind of a big luxury home or something.

After we washed up, the truck driver's office manager offered to take us to breakfast; an offer we immediately graciously accepted. We had eggs, tortillas and tamales - a really good filling breakfast at a little restaurant that actually looked like the back patio of someone's home. Little pigs wandered among the three little rickety knee-high wooden tables that were set up as a "restaurant" on about a 20 foot high rise on the west side of the roadway.

The truck then took us to the border and we got checked through the border quickly. Then we drove on again until we were within several kilometers of San Salvador, the capital of El Salvador. The guys had gone quite a bit out of their way for us and we thanked them profusely and gave them our addresses. They offered us money to help us along our way, but we declined their offer because somehow it just didn't seem right.

Soon the driver of another truck with three guys in the back pulled over for us and we hopped on. The truck took us right to a bus stop on the outskirts of San Salvador. We stood around for a while until we could get into a conversation with the driver of the next bus. We talked with him for a while and he offered us a free ride into the city.

CHAPTER 10 - EL SALVADOR

> "Most folks are about as happy as they make up their minds to be."
> Abraham Lincoln

We arrived at downtown San Salvador about noon. Just talking with some people we met, we found a guy who said he knew all about the various consulates but that they were all closed until 2:00. He suggested that we go right to the Honduras consulate and wait there until 2:00 PM, and then run over to the Nicaraguan consulate on the other side of town; and then, before 4:30, rush over to the Costa Rica consulate and finish all our paperwork with the exception of Panama.

Following his enthusiastic advice, we waited by the Honduras consulate's office until 2:30 when the consulate finally arrived. We were told that we didn't need a visa to just pass through. We rushed over to the Nicaragua consulate and found out that the Nicaragua consulate doesn't open at all in the afternoon, but it does stay open until 1:00. If we had only gone there first, we could have left right then, but since it was Friday and the consulates were closed weekends, it looked like we would have to spend the next two days in San Salvador.

We sat down outside the gate of the Nicaraguan consulate pondering our fate until Ross and I decided to walk down the street to buy some milk and bananas for lunch. After quite a while, a car drove up which we hoped was the consulate's. I ran to the gate uttering a string of broken Spanish words, hoping that out of pity they would open the door for us and give us our visas.

After some confusion I learned that they were actually Mexicans looking for the Nicaraguan consulate themselves. Fortunately, however, they knew more about the area than we did and they told us that there was a Nicaraguan consulate open on Saturday in San Miguel, another 100 miles on south. On that basis, at about 4:00 PM, we decided to head south for San Miguel, El Salvador.

We took a municipal bus to the outskirts of town, and then started "thumbing". Our first ride was in the bed of a pickup driven by a little red-headed Mexican teenager. He dropped us off at an intersection crowded with people. We decided we would have a better chance to get picked up if we separated ourselves from the crowd, so we walked down the road a quarter mile or so.

We didn't wait there long before a young graduate lawyer from San Salvador, Baltezar Hernandes, picked us up. What a blessing. He was so friendly, appeared solidly middle-class, and seemed really interested in our travels and where we came from. We rode almost to San Miguel with him. About half way there, it began raining and I asked him if there was any place we could sleep where he was going to let us off. He said "Sure," his home, and he invited us to dinner and to wash up too. We accepted his offer and he treated us very nicely. He himself served us when we were eating dinner. We had beans, rice, pineapple, tortillas, coffee and sweetbreads - all of which were very tasty. We washed up, changed socks and felt like a million. His house was very big, but very crude with a concrete floor, adobe whitewashed walls, and a tile ceiling over open rafters.

That night, Fred and I slept on army cots without blankets and we froze. We didn't think we could get up in the middle of the night and get out our sleeping bags because we would have disturbed the whole household. We were in the living room and the whole house consisted of the living room, kitchen and one bedroom.

We did our best to get some sleep on the cots until early the next morning when we got up. Ross had it worse because he was sleeping in a hammock with the cool fresh air circulating all around him. We found him that morning with two pair of pants on, two shirts and a jacket. From what he said, he slept "real cool."

*Carl and Ross at home of Baltezar Hernandes
El Salvador*

That morning, when we had to relieve ourselves, we asked for directions to the bathroom. Our friend pointed out the back door, so we headed out that way. The property appeared to be half an acre or so in size. There were no other buildings on it. We looked all around and found a bamboo mat hanging between two trees. There was human waste around the base of the trees, so we presumed we had found the "bathroom". We did what we had to and then went back into the house. We were served a hearty breakfast, thanked our host for all his kindness, and hit the road again.

Within 10 minutes of comfortable morning waiting we got a ride half way to San Miguel in a Jeep pickup.

That driver let us off at another intersection. Within half an hour the same driver came back, having completed an errand, and took us to San Miguel. I guess he felt sorry for us; that wasn't really necessary because by that time we were already feeling pretty sorry for ourselves having to do so much waiting, waiting and waiting..

We got our visas in San Miguel from a very pleasant Consulate with no problem. Leaving his office, we asked for directions back to the Pan American Highway and got several suggestions, all of which seemed to contradict each other. In any case, we took off walking toward what we expected to be the Highway, crossed to the other side of Town, got additional advice, crossed back again, and finally met two guys who offered to drive us out of town where there would only be one roadway. One of the things we were beginning to recognize was the lack of concern, or interest, the general folk had for the Pan American Highway. They knew well enough about the roads in their cities and towns, but beyond that they just didn't have much interest. Our perspective was "traveling through" and I think that made it doubly difficult for us to communicate about directions.

The two guys who offered to take us out of town to the highway were driving a nearly new car. We wondered where they had gotten the money for that, but we didn't have the rudeness to ask.

The next ride we got was with a relatively wealthy Salvadoran who also invited us into his home. There we talked about the United States for an hour or so before he invited us to use his home to shave, watch TV and listen to Paul Anka records. He couldn't seem to get enough out of us about the United States. Finally he even offered us lunch; and what a fabulous meal he served us - shrimp, steak, potatoes, french bread, beans, rice, everything plus a cold beer for me.

After stuffing ourselves as much as we politely could, we pulled all our things together and hit the road again.

Our next benefactor was a truck driver who was part owner of a bus line. He took us to his bus "terminal", gave us a written note for a pass, and told us that if we would wait there one of his company's buses would be along shortly and would take us almost to the Nicaraguan border.

We waited nearly two hours for one of his buses but none ever appeared. Finally we asked the driver of some other bus line whether we could ride with him, and he invited us without hesitation. He was interested in our story and that was good enough for him.

We had to crouch down slightly to get into the bus. As we did so we noticed that everyone on the bus was wearing or carrying a firearm of some sort - most were wearing hip holsters with pistols in them. It looked like something out of a cheap western movie that had erroneously used a modern bus in a cowboy scene that was supposed to be from a previous century. We sat near the back of the bus clutching our big green duffle bags and tried to look like we belonged there. We were probably each at least a foot taller than anyone else onboard.

The fifteen mile trip to the border was one of the slowest we had ever taken. The bus driver stopped and waited for five or ten minutes at every little wide spot in the road.

Everybody who got on the bus after us was also carrying a weapon. We did not want to ask why everyone was carrying guns, but when we got off the bus at the last stop before the Honduras border, an older gray-bearded fellow in a wide-rim cowboy hat told us that it was very bad to be near the border between El Salvador and Honduras because the governments of those two countries had some continuing disagreement about the exact location of the border and most of the people in the area carried guns to defend themselves if attacked.

The bus trip ended about ten minutes from the border at a cross roads in the middle of nowhere. Everyone seemed to know where they were going, except us. Before we knew it, we were all alone at this bump in the road in the middle of the jungle. We waited there for a while thinking we would hitch a ride with the next vehicle, until we saw four apparently drunken Salvadorans on the horizon. They were talking loudly and occasionally waving a rifle in the air. All we had to defend ourselves in case of an altercation was our pocket knives, so we started walking south.

We walked faster and farther with those bags that evening than I think we ever walked on the whole trip. We actually believed that our lives were in danger, although we never got close enough to the guys to really know. They kept talking and shouting and occasionally waving their arms, and we kept walking. We were separated by about the length of a football field or so.

We walked as fast as we could until a Volkswagen Microbus driven by a local fisherman stopped to pick us up. He drove us to the border, which was just a fence into the jungle with a big wooden gate and a little guardhouse on the side - *Oficina de Migración el Amatillo*. There was no place to sleep on the Salvadoran side and we didn't want to just sleep in the jungle, so we paid the after hours fee to cross the border, and crossed into Nicaragua. There were forty or fifty people on the Nicaraguan side of the border, all hanging around a couple of portable bar-b-ques. It was pretty dark by then but we still didn't feel like hanging around the border, so we began asking around for a ride.

Several of the guys standing around told us that the two big "Soyfe" trucks that were parked in the area were going all the way to Costa Rica. They pointed out the drivers to us and we went over to ask them if we could hitch a ride. They were the most surly guys we had met so far. They acted like we weren't worth talking to and they didn't want to be bothered. We persisted, trying to make small talk with them and disregarding the fact that we were being ignored. After fifteen or twenty minutes of one-sided conversation, they finally decided to acknowledge us. They told us they could take us to within 20 miles of Managua for $5 each. We told them we couldn't afford to spend that kind of money on that short a leg of the trip, but there was no flexibility in them, and we couldn't make a deal.

CHAPTER 11 - HONDURAS

> "Men and nations act rationally once they have exhausted all other alternatives."
> Abba Eban

We slept uneasily that night at the border patrol station in Honduras. The station had three rooms and they let us sleep in one of them. Fred slept on an overturned blackboard placed across two benches, on top of his sleeping bag which was still leaking a lot of feathers. He nearly froze. Ross and I slept on the floor. We were all very happy late the next morning when we got a ride in a big open flat-bed truck to a little town at the intersection of the Pan American Highway and the road northeast to Tegucigalpa where the driver dropped us off and headed on to Tegucigalpa.

Honduras seemed like the most uncivilized, most backward country we had ever seen, and it sure wasn't very good for hitchhikers either; no traffic. That morning, with the only Honduras money we had, we bought two packages of pastries which we ate with water. That was our breakfast. We waited on the outskirts of town; and, even there, miles from the border, about half the men we saw were wearing sidearms.

Around 11 AM the driver of an empty dump truck invited us to hop on. That truck carried us to the next town and as we drove into town some drunk came out of the town's only gas station waving a gun over his head and shouting and shooting into the air. No one paid any attention. Somebody handed him bottle of beer; he leaned up against a pole, started guzzling and with one more errant shot into the air, that was the end of the ruckus.

We waited at the edge of town in the very hot sun until about noon when a Singer sewing machine salesman rode by in his truck. He gave us a ride to a town that was within half an hour of the Nicaraguan border. We walked around the town center a bit and spotted what looked like a very nice restaurant where we decided to have an early dinner. We each got a fabulous steak for about 40 cents including dessert! As we left town, we met a Nicaraguan hitchhiker who was on his way home. He was a photographer who had been trying his luck in Honduras but who had concluded that the Hondurans were not yet far enough past the nomadic food gathering stage to provide him with the standard of living he wished to attempt to maintain. He joined us and temporarily we became a group of four.

The four of us waited until almost nightfall when a bus passed by and offered to take us to the border for a small price. We gave up our hitching and paid the few cents he was asking for the ride. There was so little traffic where we were that we were afraid we could wait weeks before getting a lift. We got to a town just short of the border at about 8:00 p.m. and got invited to spend the night at the police station.

We walked that evening downtown to get a dinner of French bread, sardines, peaches and avocados. The police fixed us up some makeshift bunks in one of the rooms of the station house. I slept on two benches placed together. Fred slept on another blackboard. Ross slept on a piece of plywood, and our Nicaraguan buddy slept on a cot.

The next morning we said good-bye to our Honduran police force hosts, crossed the border, and got out on the road to start hitching again. Within minutes a very nice fellow stopped to pick us up and offered to take us right to Managua. Before we could climb into his truck, the Nicaraguan border police came over to ask what he was doing. He attempted to explain what was going on but the officers insisted that picking up riders in Nicaragua was illegal and that if he gave us a ride we would all be arrested. The driver apologized profusely to the policemen and drove off without us. We found the local bus station and paid the required fare to get to Managua.

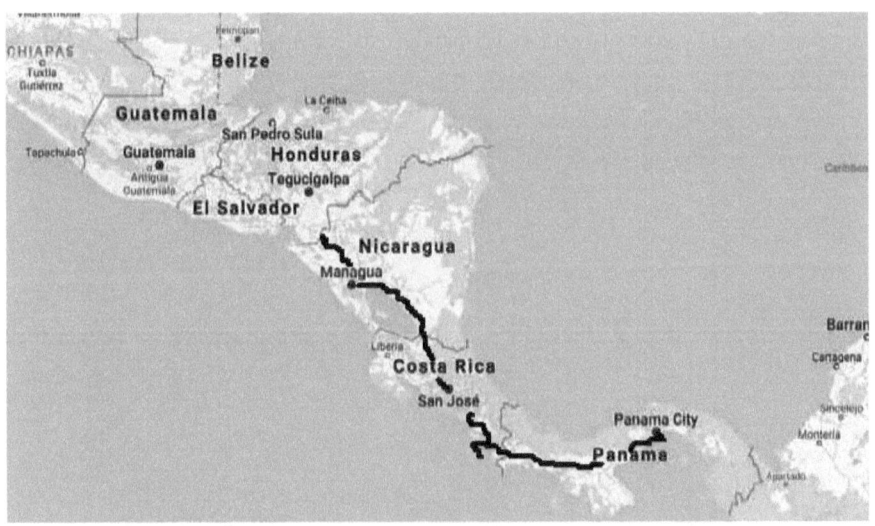
Approximate route from Nicaragua to Panama
Map data ©2018 Google, INEGI

CHAPTER 12 - NICARAGUA

> "With few exceptions, the less you know about the cause of a problem, the easier it is for you to believe that you know the solution to it."
> Author unknown

Our bus pulled into Managua at about 1 pm. We quickly found the Costa Rican consulate but it had closed at noon. We walked around the block and rented two small rooms in a very well kept little hostel for three American dollars. The people there were very nice. They moved in an extra bed for us without a charge so we all three slept on beds that night after having nice showers and a good beef steak dinner for the three of us for about a $1.10 each.

We got up at about nine the next morning only to face one of the biggest crises of the trip. Fred wanted to turn back. I was tired of traveling too and just about agreed with him. We were very tired. We had found few friends since our lawyer friend in El Salvador, and we had spent nearly half of our money.

Ross wanted to continue and he offered to lend Fred $15, which gave Fred the money he needed to continue. Fred had less money left than I did. Ross' loan seemed to save the day for the time being.

Our next stop was to be Costa Rica. We had heard that it was the most progressive of all Latin American countries because of its Social Democratic government patterned after Sweden. We had also heard that there was no army there and that fewer than 20 percent of the people were illiterate; whereas in the other countries of Central American illiteracy at that time was about 70 percent. Costa Rico sounded like something to see, but we all agreed that we would have to cut Panama out of our plans for sure if we spent any time in Costa Rica because it would just cost us too much.

According to Ross's book, "Traveling Latin America", we figured that it would cost us about $25.00 more to go to Costa Rica than it would to start returning home from right where we were. If we did go to Costa Rica, I would have about $115.00 left to get back to the States, Fred would have less, and Ross never seemed to be concerned about the money. It didn't really seem worth it but since we had come so far already we finally convinced ourselves to go the extra miles.

We lugged the bags from our comfortable "*pension*" to a little restaurant where we each had a fairly good-sized breakfast. Then we lugged them a good half mile more to the Pan American highway, where we stood for about ten minutes watching traffic going both north and south. Every inch south we went was just an inch more we had to come back, we said to each other.

At that point I said, "Let's forget Costa Rica, let's go home..." Fred kind of agreed and we started to cross to the east side of the highway to try to flag down a northbound ride. Ross was frustrated with us for being so double minded, and as we were crossing the road he complained impatiently: "Well, what do you guys want to do?!"

We hadn't altogether crossed the road when a big semi heading north pulled off the gravel road onto the shoulder toward which we were carrying our bags. We moved to avoid the semi and got ourselves half way out in the middle of the road just as a bus headed south pulled over to pick some people up on that side of the road. The driver thought we had stepped out in front of him to stop him so we could get on his bus. He stopped and waved us across the street thinking we wanted to get on his bus. For an instant we didn't know what we were doing. Ross waved back a "thank you" to the bus driver; we glanced at one another, grabbed our bags, and we were on our way to Costa Rica on the bus!

We got on the bus knowing that, although we had some traveler's checks, we lacked the cash to be able to pay for the ride. We worried about that nearly to the Costa Rican border when the conductor finally came to the back of the bus to collect. When we gave him what we had and told him we had no more, he shrugged off the short-change as though it were nothing. That was about the third conductor who had shrugged off our short change without a complaint. We resolved from that point on to short change all the buses drivers. We were pretty arrogant young men when it came to presuming what others owed us for being alive.

Here are some notes from Fred's recollections of "the crisis":

> Our crisis was real, but fortunately it was resolved through the generosity of my kind companions. I surely wanted to make it to our longstanding goal of Panama, and felt really bad about ruining the rest of our trip, but funds were becoming a serious issue, meaning I had almost none. Because I had zero family support, my college days were spent in perpetual insolvency, and I was becoming seriously concerned about having enough money for the coming college year (a pretty standard condition for me). Although I was a full-fledged California resident, had spent the last three years in California, graduated from a California high school, and was 100% financially independent, the University of California couldn't believe that total financial independence was possible or legitimate for a young college student, so I had to pay the expensive out-of-state tuition (my parents had left me behind and moved from California to Colorado in my Senior year) which added a substantial burden to my costs. It was grossly unfair, and I complained, but no one would listen. A few years later someone in my position sued the University and won, but far too late for

me. What was pocket change for most college students often was my entire earthly store.

My overall situation meant I had to work long and hard hours in my college days, but I don't regret that because there were interesting and useful experiences along the way. I really should have been working that summer instead of traveling, but the call of the road had been too strong.

It's worth mentioning that Ross' loaning me the money was very much a reflection of his nature. He was a very generous person, and often went out of his way to help others. His whole family lived their faith, which became mine also, and that was one thing that had attracted me to it.

So, while I was surprised by and never expected Ross' help, it wasn't a strange thing for him to do, and happily for us all it meant "The Trip" didn't come to an inglorious end right there in Managua.

CHAPTER 13 - COSTA RICA

> "Men do not attract that which they want, but that which they are."
> James Allen, British philosophical writer

We got to the Costa Rican border at about 8:00 p.m. The border officers wanted us to hurry across so that they could close up. Because it was after 5 pm we would have to pay another late fee. We asked one of the officers how much late fee would be and when he said "one dollar each" we asked him where we could sleep on his side of the border in Nicaragua. So far, the trip from San Diego had cost us about $35.00 each and every dollar was precious. We slept in a hallway at the border crossing office with smoke from some half-drowned wood fire blowing over our noses all night. As soon as I woke up the next morning I began sneezing.

We had to wait two hours after we awoke in the morning for the border to open; so, lacking anything else to do, with rain outside, and smoke inside, I continued my sneezing. That sneezing developed into a full fledged cold in the next few days.

When the rain let up we crossed the border and met a truck driver who was going south to San Jose. We asked for a ride and he invited us to ride along. We wanted to get moving so badly that we didn't bother to ask how much it would cost; instead Fred and I just climbed under the canvas tarp that covered the bed of the truck while Ross climbed into the cab. Ross had taken the interpersonal relations lead role for us, and we were happy to have him do it. He loved to talk and people seemed to enjoy talking with him. He had an easy smile and a good sense of humor which seemed to make people feel comfortable. We rode all the way to San Jose trouble-free, except for a thunder storm which made driving difficult for a part of the trip.

Halfway to San Jose the driver, Señor Cordera, bought us each two big glasses of *cafe-con-leche* (that's coffee with milk and it's mixed about half and half and is really delicious) and two really meaty sandwiches. He also went hog wild at some mango stand, I really didn't love mangos at the time, and bought us each about five mangos which we ate to be courteous. As we drove, rain filled the top of the tarp in places with ponds of water so that before long it couldn't be lifted off the sidewalls of the flatbed. Ross and the driver couldn't get in and we couldn't get out. They fed us like birds in a cage. Surprising to me, even though it was summer, the water everywhere made my feet freeze and I was chilly all day.

The other problem we had was the bugs! Thousands and thousands of bugs of all sorts were in the back of the truck with us. At one point when I attempted to talk to Fred I opened my mouth and a butterfly flew in! We each got stung once and spent a lot of the trip brushing bugs off ourselves.

We got to Señor Cordera's home in Herida, Costa Rica, at about 6:00 PM. By that time Ross had made pretty good friends with him and when Fred and I climbed out of the back of the flatbed we found that he had invited us in for dinner. And what a dinner that was!! They served us everything from appetizers to dinner wine and it was delicious! We ate like hyenas, but we were hungry!

After dinner we sat around and they told us all about Costa Rica and how much they loved their country. We began to wonder where we were going to sleep that night when he told us that he would be glad to let us stay the night with them. There were four kids in his family and they were all very kind and friendly. I had never known a truck driver's family before and I had not expected them to be so kind.

We slept on mattresses on the floor and slept better than we had slept in a week. The next day they fed us a huge breakfast and pointed us toward the center of town and the bank. Because the trip had cost us so little from Managua to San Jose (about $1.50 each), and because our new found friend told us that there was plenty of work for Americans in Panama, we decided to continue on to Panama after we took some time to rest and clean up in San Jose.

Our first stop in San Jose after the bank was the office of the Panamanian consulate. He told us that the road was passable to Panama, and he was sure we could make the trip by bus for less than $10.00 each. By that time I had developed a head cold and didn't feel very well at all, and all of our clothes were filthy so we began to look for a place to stay for a few days.

In Mexico City we had chanced to meet an American lady whose son, Benjamin Morris, was an exchange student from Kansas, who she told us was studying in Costa Rica. She also told us that, if we ever got to Costa Rica, we should stop in to see him. Bennie seemed our best bet at the moment, and because we didn't have an address or anything, we just started hiking toward the University to see if we would be able to find him.

As we approached the university campus we were stopped at a red light where we had to wait for the stop light to change color. A girl who looked like a Costa Rican approached the corner and began waiting next to us. I asked her if she could help us find the university (I had a pretty good idea where it was, but we were all getting tired carrying our bags - they seemed so heavy! - and she looked over at us as though she expected us to ask for some kind of help, so I asked).

Noemi happened to be fluent in English and it was fun to be able to communicate so well with a stranger again. She helped us look for Ben and also for a room in one of the dormitories.

The students were on vacation and none of the university

offices were open that day. Ben wasn't listed in the telephone directory. We walked to a *"Pension Estudiante,"* and several other places that housed students and found neither Ben nor a room to rent.

By late afternoon Noemi was beginning to get interested in us. She told us about a place not far from the University where we could get a good cheap meal, and probably find a good place to stay. Then she switched subjects a bit and told us that there were lots of girls there, not good girls, but pretty girls; and she noted that she was a good girl. She said she wouldn't even go into the neighborhood where she was about to send us. We told her that we liked good girls, and we didn't necessarily want to go where she was thinking of sending us.

When we got to the bus stop where she was going to send us off she casually mentioned that her house in Santa Ana was just outside of town and we could probably stay there, but "it would be too modest for Americans to stay in." We struggled to convince her that we were sure her place would be very nice and that we would love to stay with her and her family. She told us she would have to ask her mother about us and gave us her phone number and told us to call her in a couple of hours.

We wandered around the University, picked up a local newspaper, and just tried to pass the time after she left. Fred and Ross each bought shirts to replace the filthy ones they had abandoned in Mexico City.

Our phone call was tense until she said "Mom says fine, you can stay as long as you like". We could have screamed for joy. At her house I could recover from my cold; we could all get cleaned up; and we would have some local friends! That phone call was a wonderful dream come true for us! We bought some flowers for Noemi to get things started off right. Fred picked them out and ended up carrying them in one hand while his bag was in the other. We got some giggles from passers-by but we were happy to be going to a home and a few giggles didn't hurt too much.

Noemi had a slightly older sister and an eleven year old brother, Freddie. When we got to their house they insisted on washing our clothes for us and they let us take showers. They fed us a good meal with a great bean dish.

Noemi and her family were all very friendly to us and we had a lot of fun with them. They all have great senses of humor, although sometimes it took us a while to get the punch line of a joke when the whole story line is about Latin American cultural things - and the translation of the language itself makes our understanding of jokes told to us in Spanish a bit complicated.

They told us they were Methodists, not Catholics like the majority of their neighborhood. A lot of homes in their neighborhood had signs in their windows saying: "We are Catholics and we don't accept Protestant propaganda."

They gave us an office, or den, to sleep in. The room had a couple of nicely upholstered chairs, a couch, a desk, a typewriter, and a short wave radio as well as a stereo console with a large collection of long-play classical music albums, including a bunch of Strauss pieces. It was a very comfortable nice room with a mattress on the floor and we felt very much at home.

The morning after we arrived we were surprised to read in the newspaper that Guatemala had just had an aborted coup-d-etat. A fellow in the neighborhood told us that the communists have a good chance of winning elections in Costa Rica, and another told us that the Russians would soon be the leaders of the world. We heard that the United States was giving some millions of dollars to the government of Nicaragua, but the locals in the neighborhood complained that they thought that money would just go to line the pockets of the government officials.

We were told that in Costa Rica there is no army, only local police. That sounded great to us because that way the money that would otherwise be spent on military personnel and hardware could be spent on schools, roads, hospitals and other needed public facilities. That is in contrast to the millions spent in Nicaragua, Honduras and El Salvador to fight with each other. Noemi's college cost her about US$60 a year as opposed to ours which cost around $1,000 with room, board, travel, and tuition. She was surprised to know that our schooling cost so much.

To our surprise, in the evenings it was pretty chilly in San Jose; cold enough to not feel comfortable with the windows open. That turned out to be a problem for us because my cold went from my respiratory area to my intestines and by the time we were ready to turn in that evening I was having some pretty significant flatulence. It got worse as the night came on and Ross and Fred got pretty upset with me about it for a while.

CHAPTER 14 - NOEMI'S

>"I never eat more than I can lift."
>Miss Piggy of the Muppets

Noemi's house was one in a row of houses. The very front room was the room we had been given. It was like an extra bedroom or a study. The entry for the house was in the living room, which was adjacent to our room. Then there was a country kitchen, and in the rear of the house were three bedrooms two on one side of the bathroom, and one on the other. Noemi's Mother had one of the bedrooms, Freddie had another, and Noemi and her sister slept in the other one. They were all in the back part of the house.

Through the night I kept having to get up to use the bathroom. The house and the neighborhood were quiet as a tomb at night and I tried so hard not to make any bathroom sounds. It was so embarrassing; but after a while for me, Ross, and Fred, it became a gigglefest. We were always so tired, and had expected to finally get a couple of good nights of sleep. Being kept awake all night for this became just too much. Like a bunch of little kids at a pajama party, when I would experience a digestive upset, I would start to laugh. Then Fred; then Ross. They must have thought that Americans were really something strange.

It was terrible for us; the odors were unbearable. Ross kept trying to fan the air around in the room to get it out, but then he started having gas too. We finally just gave up, while poor Fred lay collapsed on his mattress. We were almost afraid to open the door the first morning that we were there because the smell was so bad and we couldn't figure out how to operate the window latch to open the windows. Somehow we survived that night and in the morning we got up bright and early and opened the front door! I know they thought we were crazy by that time, so we thought we might as well just get down to the basics, like oxygen, and forget about the niceties for the time being. Maybe the next night we would be all better and everyone would forget about our first night in San Jose.

As soon as Noemi came into the room that first morning she suggested that we open the windows because she said it would get hot inside during the day. She was very proper and respectful.

Noemi's family treated us like kings, even though we had these digestive problems. Ross and I were in the kitchen the evening of the second day doing the dishes and I had gas all day, but we had been out and around a lot and I hadn't been specifically embarrassed by it.

Anyway, Noemi was in the kitchen ironing while we were doing the dishes. I presumed she was aware of my problem when it occurred again and it would just be ignored. She was a very refined girl, and I knew she wouldn't embarrass someone on purpose, but, when I had the problem, she noticed the odor and asked me and Ross whether we smelled a bad smell. I kind of ducked behind him and tried not to look or pay any attention.

Thinking her house might have some functional problem, she asked again "Did you smell anything funny?" and I said "I don't know"; and she persisted: "Are you sure?" All the while she was opening pots and closets and sniffing, and then Ross and I exchanged glances and began laughing. Then I think Noami recognized what that meant and she conveniently walked out of the room. I felt like some great secret had been discovered of me and I was so embarrassed. I thought I was the bad one until Ross told me that he was the one having the problems and then we both started laughing our heads off. I don't think she ever asked us again whether we smelled anything bad because we always had digestive problems with the food. We complicated that on the third day when we got up about eight o'clock in the morning to have breakfast.

That morning the family decided to go out to do some shopping and Ross decided to join them. By this time, he was spending as much time with Noemi as he could and they seemed to be having a great time together. Fred and I were happy to stay home and relax. We talked about poverty and riches and why we had what we did, and the Costa Ricans had what they did, and so forth. To my mind the only way to express it was to say that: The United States is a Miracle! We talked about it a bit with Noami. She had a favorite expression in English for it: Such is Life.

CHAPTER 15 - OJO DE AGUA

"All happy families are alike; each unhappy family is unhappy in its own way."
Leo Tolstoy

July 15, 1961
I had about $85 left in travelers checks and was trying to really squeeze my money when Ross came in and told us that he had arranged a day trip for us all to go to a botanical park and a swimming place west of the city. It was going to cost us each a dollar. Fred and I were both beginning to try to kind of hoard our money and we got to calling Ross the "Americano Rico". Anyway, that day we went to the Ojo de Agua to go swimming.

Costa Rican five colones bill in use in the 1960s

Ojo de Agua is a beautiful park built around a fresh water spring that generates more than 5,000 gallons a minute on the outskirts of San Jose. It is a really beautiful park.

Noami expected us to get really excited about it, but we didn't get that awfully excited. It was pretty and all that, nice to look at. I didn't go swimming in it, although it was really attractive, because I had a little cold and I wanted to get rid of it before I got another chill. Ross went in and from that time Ross and Noami really got to be good friends. After the swim we walked around, wasted time till finally around five o'clock when we went back home.

That evening when we were just about to sit down for dinner Noemi's father knocked on the door. Noemi's father and mother had been divorced for four or five years. We didn't know much about her father, or their family relationships, but he offered to take us to a party at the home of one of his friends so that we "could learn about Costa Rica." We agreed, and that started a heated argument between Noami, her mother her father about who should go where with whom. We couldn't understand much of their conversation because it was such fast spoken Spanish, but it made us feel a little uncomfortable, even though we felt like we would like to go to a Costa Rican party.

Later we learned that they were telling him not to get us into any trouble. He apparently had become quite a drinker, and some of the women he spent time with were not of the moral character of Noemi and her mother. By now Noemi's mother was treating us like we were her boys, and she didn't want anything bad to happen to us.

In any case, we ended up going to the party and it was just a drunken type of thing. We sat around keeping pretty much to ourselves, even though the women at the party tried to be very friendly to us.

At one point someone passed Ross a glass of beer which he thought was soda. As soon as he tasted it he grimaced and put it down someplace. We were dressed in blue jeans, or khakis, and tennis shoes, so our clothing didn't fit in very well either. At one point a rather inviting looking woman tripped over someone's foot and almost dumped a tray of beer mugs on my lap. I told Fred that I wished she had because it would have given us an excuse to leave.

Ross contributed something to the festivities by singing "Home on the Range," and some other old folk songs to the great pleasure of the group. Everyone seemed to enjoy his singing even though he forgot some of the words and just made up unintelligible sounds to cover over the missing words.

We spent an hour or so sipping sodas, until finally Noami broke out crying. What a terrible thing that party turned out to be. I really never understood what was going on but, apparently, the sight of her own father whooping it up with these women who could have been school classmates of hers made her very upset.

Noemi told us that her oldest sister had gotten pregnant before she got married, and then shortly after the baby was born, she got a divorce.   Noemi's father and her sister's ex-husband made this family feel that men weren't very good people. I think they appreciated us because of the values we seemed to have. Their family was very sad. It was so distressing to see Noemi crying.

Ross was really was moved by Noemi's sadness and wanted to do whatever he could to help. In one corner of the room he started trying to teach her about his religion so that she could see how that would lead to having a more perfect marriage. Fred and I offered whatever casual advice we could think of and tried to make light of the situation so that we could all move on to something else.

Ross wouldn't give up trying to counsel Noemi, and I told him I thought he was playing football with an eggshell because it looked like he was trying to make her fall for him. He wasn't paying any attention to me by that time.

When Noemi's dad drove us home, he wanted to drop Noemi off and take us back to the party with him. We all declined and separated to our rooms.

The next morning we began to make plans for the next step of our trip. Fred and I were ready to continue our travels the next day; Ross said he would be happy to just get to know Noemi and Costa Rica better. Fred and I made some effort to talk him on to Panama, but that was fruitless at that point, so Fred and I planned our departure, and

Ross started following the family's schedule as though he was one of them full-time.

Fred and I slept in on what was supposed to be our last full day at Noemi's. I was finally getting over my cold and Fred just wanted to sleep late. When the family planned an early shopping trip that day, Ross got up early to go along with them. That left me and Fred alone at breakfast.

Corn Flakes were not a staple in Costa Rica; in fact, they were sold in little cans about the size of the cans we used for hot chocolate. Noemi's Mom had a can of corn flakes in one of the kitchen closets, which Fred and I had been eyeing since we were first invited to wash and put away the dishes. For some reason, since we had left the United States, we had a powerful craving for Corn Flakes, and we didn't have the courage to ask for the little can of flakes when Noemi's Mom made breakfast for us each morning.

Being alone, however, our true selves came forward - and, when it came to Corn Flakes, we were just plain depraved. We got up that morning, shaved and got dressed and set ourselves up for a Corn Flakes orgy - with that little can of corn flakes as our centerpiece, and a bottle of milk, and the sugar bowl on either side.

When everything was on the table, we served ourselves - first the Flakes, then the milk - and milk was a pretty revered commodity in that household also - and, finally, the topping of a good coating of sugar from the sugar bowl.

I told Fred that I had resisted as much as I could and I was going to eat a big bowl of corn flakes and drink a whole bottle of milk. I didn't care what the consequences were, I was just desperate to have a big bowl of corn flakes!

We poured our corn flakes and then I dumped half the bottle of milk on mine. I took a big heaping spoonful of sugar from the bowl that was on the table, and dumped at least three heaping spoonfuls on the corn flakes! Then I plunged the large serving spoon I had set on the table for myself into the corn flakes, opened my mouth wide in anticipation of enjoying the wonderful sweet familiar taste of a fresh bowl of corn flakes, and AAHHHHHCHHHCHTT!!!! YUK!!! YUK!!! YUK!!!!

I spit out the corn flakes in an instant and looked at my giant bowl of corn flakes with a disbelieving stare. THIS CANNOT BE HAPPENING!!!! THIS CANNOT BE HAPPENING!!! THIS IS TOO TERRIBLE TO BE CONCEIVED OF AS HAPPENING!!! I HAD DUMPED THREE HEAPING TABLESPOONS OF SALT ON MY CORN FLAKES!!! WHAT TO DO NOW!!!! WHAT TO DO?!?!!!

Fred could see that something was wrong, but couldn't imagine yet what it was.

SALT!!

SALT!!!

THAT WAS SALT I PUT ON MY CORN FLAKES!!!

EEEEYYUUCKKKK!!! IT'S TERRIBLE!!!!!

Fred started to laugh but then caught himself because he realized the same thing could have happened to him - the salt bowl and the sugar bowl looked almost exactly the alike.

I was not going to allow this to stand. I would not let capricious fate deal me that bad a hand. I would over come it; I would conquer this challenge; and so, I set about doing just that.

I found a small empty bowl in the kitchen. I carefully skimmed as many of the salt crystals that hadn't already dissolved off the top of the corn flakes and milk. Then I found the sugar bowl and dumped three heaping spoonfuls of sugar on top of the whole mess and dug in for a second try with my over-sized serving spoon. UGH! What a terrible tasting concoction, but I wasn't about to give up.

I forced one spoon after another of that disgusting mess down my gullet even though my stomach had attempted to refuse it from the first taste.

TOO BAD STOMACH!!! I'M GOING TO EAT THIS STUFF IF IT KILLS ME BECAUSE I AM NOT GOING TO LET ALL THOSE PRECIOUS CORN FLAKES AND THAT EXTRA PRECIOUS MILK GO TO WASTE!!! THAT'S JUST THE WAY IT IS; SO, STOMACH, GET WITH THE PROGRAM - START DIGESTING!

I have since learned how futile it is to mentally direct your stomach to do something that it is not built to do. Of all of the digestive mistakes I have ever made in my life, there is none that looms larger than this one because, not only did I feel totally sick from my toes to my fingertips to the top of my head for the next two days from force feeding myself that crap, but the results of my indigestion inflicted incalculable discomfort upon my associates and the family that was hosting us.

That night was a night none of us will ever forget. The unwelcome sounds and smells began in the evening and rarely during the entire night were there sixty minutes that were not punctuated by their interruption. It was literally the worst night of my life, and probably close to that for all those in the house with me.

"Are we in the septic tank cleaning business?" I asked myself that night. "No," I answered, "we just smell that way." I started having gas within an hour after finishing that horrid breakfast and it just kept getting worse until the next morning.

I spent the late afternoon and evening alone in my room with the little window propped open. At about 8:00 in the evening Fred came in and almost passed out. A minute was about all he could take. He left the room and sent the rest of them to check on me because they couldn't understand why he didn't want to sleep in his room that night. Minutes after he left, our door squeaked open and three little Costa Rican heads peeked in, for a second. Then they all started laughing their heads off. Even Señora Alvarado, when she looked in the doorway, held her nose and spoke in the funniest sounding Spanish.

What she was doing was invoking the emergency response plan, which involved opening all the windows and installing a fan to keep the air moving in a southward direction through our room and out to the street. I could do nothing but just keep gassing away.

Señora Alvarado decided that no one could sleep in the same room with me so they moved Fred in with Freddie, laughing like mad all the time. At that point, this experience with these "*gringos*" was just too funny to be even embarrassing to anyone.

The bathroom I had to use was located between the two bedrooms occupied by the host family members, and the room occupied by Ross. There is no way my apologies could compensate for the pain I inflicted upon them, but they were all so compassionate. I deserved what I got for being so selfish with the cornflakes and milk, but heaven knows the family and my two buddies did nothing to deserve what they got. What A Night!

All night long I kept burping - oh, the most horrible taste - and going to the bathroom. Ross and Fred were sleeping in rooms right off the bathroom so they didn't escape it all. I really was sick. In the middle of the night Ross felt a little seriously concerned about me.

Carl, how are you doing?

Oh, my God, Ross, I am only three feet tall and I feel as badly as I smell!

That brief conversation elicited chuckles from *everyone* even though it was someplace between two and three in the morning when we all should have been asleep!

In the morning Freddie, Noemi's twelve year old brother, came into my room, took the diving mask and snorkel from my duffle bag, put it on and told me that I should have put it on with the snorkel out the window to get some fresh air to breathe. At least they all seemed to have a good sense of humor about the situation.

We decided to stay another day so I could recover. The afternoon of our last day we took a day trip to one of the local inactive volcanoes around San Jose. The drive up was beautiful with clouds hanging in the sky below us and the tremendous distance views we got. It rained and got quite cold, but the trip was worthwhile anyway. There was some family sadness associated with this little trip too.

Noemi stayed home that morning when the rest of the family went downtown for the day. The volcano trip had been set up by her father and she didn't want to miss that time with us, and she also wanted to see the volcano. However, when her father showed up he told her she couldn't go because the trip would be too difficult for her, and she had housework to do. We learned that the real reason he didn't want to take her was that he had his mistress with him and Noemi and his mistress did not get along. Needless to say, we did not have a good impression of Noemi's father and there was an emotional chill on the visit to the volcano.

Fred and I had been planning to leave that day, but Señora Alvarado wanted to help me get better before we left so she prepared some type of lemon based remedy for me to drink all day instead of eating regular meals.

That afternoon Ross and Noami went to the library where Noemi worked and in the evening we all went downtown to see San Jose's central park. Noemi was so excited about showing us another attraction of her homeland, but, like at other times, when we got there, things just didn't go as planned. The beautiful black swans were lost in the darkness, and, for the same reason, we could hardly see the treasured "white parrots of San Jose." We were tired but we followed her all over till we came to the fountains in rainbow colored waters which she assured us we could see even better at night. It was cold. There was an old custodian sloshing around in the water with some crummy old Latin American type broom cleaning the whole place out - probably the only time it had been cleaned in years.

At that point, Fred and I were really ready to leave. At the library we found out that to get to Panama from San Jose there were 39 rivers to cross, and there was very little commercial traffic on that stretch of the highway. We rode home in a typical Costa Rican bus, which is like one of our old fashioned school buses, and when we got home we gave the local airline a ring.

It would only cost $7.00 to fly from San Jose to Palmar Sur, which was a little town about 150 miles north of David, Panama. We decided to take that plane at 5:05 a.m. the next morning and then to hitchhike to David; then catch a $5.00 bus to Panama City. We had the whole thing figured out way beforehand. We knew just what we were doing.

"Mama" made us some sandwiches from pineapple jam and peanut butter, and the next morning we set out. We made one last effort to convince Ross to come along with us, but he was feeling too comfortable in his current situation and told us he'd meet us back at college in a month.

Ross ended up staying in Costa Rica with the Alvarados for two more weeks. By that time he was considering staying indefinitely, but he had no means of earning a living - and he was driven to get his college degree. He flew back to Guatemala; took a bus to El Paso where he attended a church convention, and then got a ride with another conventioneer to El Cajon.

Fred and I got to the airport very early the next morning and the plane was a little late, so we were fine.

CHAPTER 16 - GOLFITO

"Badges... badges... we have no badges... I
don't have to show you any stinking badges!"
<u>The</u> <u>Treasure</u> <u>of</u> <u>the</u> <u>Sierra</u> <u>Madre</u>, B. Traven

The view from the plane was thrilling. We landed in Palmar Sur at about 6:30 am, walked out to the highway, and had all day to hitch a ride to David.

Not one vehicle went by for the first two hours. We waited and waited. Finally one car went by, heading north. Then another. Hours went by and it rained a little, so we got out our ponchos out again. A third vehicle drove by, also heading north, and it's driver slowed down to look us over and leaned out the window to ask what we were doing. We told him what we were up to and he looked at us and with some dismay told us that "There are no cars going from here to David. It will take you a very long time. Why don't you take the train? That would be a good business for you."

We thanked him for his concern but told him that we just didn't have the money. He drove off and wished us good luck. We stayed there till midday, and then walked back to the airport to ask about the train. We were fortunate in that the train was leaving for Golfito in the next hour and the station was less than two miles away.

We checked our map. Golfito was certainly in the direction that we were headed, so we hustled on over to the train station and talked our way onto a free ride to Golfito. Whooopee!! We did it again! We talked our way through a bind and on we chugged to Golfito, Costa Rica - heading to Panama! We were so pleased with ourselves! What macho adventurers we were! We rode second class, on wooden slat seats again, but who cares when you're riding on a free pass!

The train wasn't bad. It was a typical Banana Company

(United Fruit Company) train that traveled at a slow chug and stopped anywhere someone in the passing jungle or banana plantations waved it down. We learned that in this part of the world the Banana Company owned the trains, and a lot of other capital equipment like the docks and the ships and the houses and just about everything substantial that you saw. When we pulled into Golfito in the late afternoon we felt like a couple of celebrities stepping off the train with our big green canvas bags.

There wasn't much choice about where to go because there was only one road at the train station and it went parallel to the tracks to the north, and then just kind of dipped out of sight to the south. To the east of the tracks was Golfito Bay and to the west was a rise that could barely be called a hill that ran approximately parallel to the train tracks.

We started hiking southward and in a block or two encountered a ten foot high chain link and barbed wire fence penetrated by a gate which was overlooked by a guard station. Innocently we walked up to the guard station, because we wanted to go south. The scene quickly changed from your Emperor Jones to your Grapes of Wrath because it turned out we were nowhere!

Really. It took us a while to understand the guard, but after repeated questioning through our disbelief, we finally found out that not only doesn't the Pan American Highway, or any highway, run through Golfito, but there is no way in or out of Golfito except by plane, boat, or train - and the train only runs twice a week - and it was done running today.

To a couple of "A" students from a reputable college in the United States of America this just wasn't possible. We could not get on a train and end up nowhere! Somebody else, somebody stupid, could get on a train heading to Panama and end up nowhere, but not us. We were the celebrities who just triumphantly negotiated ourselves into a free train ride toward our destination, not a couple of duds who didn't have the brains to ask where the train we had gotten on would be able to take us. It was raining, and we were not happy. The train was gone. The next boat scheduled for Golfito, the United Fruit Company's Heredia, wouldn't be back from its run to New York for a week. The entire town was about a block wide and, except for the area beyond the gate, looked like a poor little jungle slum.

The good news for us was that the chain-linked area was the "American Compound" and, because we were Americans, the guard at the gate allowed us to pass thru. When they made that rule I don't think they particularly had us in mind, but we showed the guard our passports and the rules were the rules. He pointed us in the direction of the United Fruit Company's offices and told us we could get something to eat there.

At the Compound offices our arrival was announced by the clerk to the manager. We were asked to wait upstairs in the dining room where the manager would meet us, which he did after half an hour or so.

What a deal he made us! He was Costa Rican but he worked for the Fruit Company. His job was to host American visitors, so he told us he was our host. He invited us to dinner that evening in that beautiful dining room and told us he had a cabin for us that we were welcome to stay in until we decided to travel on. He had his staff show us to our cabin, which was a beautiful little house a hundred feet or so from the main office building, with all the amenities of home - beautiful clean sheets, a little kitchen and dining room and beautiful big windows on all sides. It was painted a pale green outside, and pale yellow within and I felt like I could have stayed there forever - raised my family there. It was lovely.

We showered and shaved and went back over to the office complex for dinner. There was only one other person in the dining room when we got there, so we went over and asked if he would mind if we joined him. He was a British student who had been traveling through Europe and Africa, then through South America. He had flown in that morning on a Fruit Company airplane and was flying north with them the next day. This guy made us look like a couple of paupers. His name was Christopher and he had been traveling for two years with no money - he just talked people out of rooms, dinners and travel as he went; and he sure looked healthy.

We all had huge steak dinners and continued exchanging stories until late in the night. This Britisher had no fear and he was traveling like a king; what stories he had to tell. Some people just seem to get up on the world and climb all over it, while the rest of us desperately cling to our little places somewhere within its bowels. Fred and I were both more than a little jealous of this guy, but at the same time in awe.

In any case, we had a great evening with Christopher. He had come up from Chile and wanted to know what to expect as he went north and through Mexico. His goal was San Francisco, after which he thought he just might head back to England.

The next morning we took a walk through a part of the American Compound and got invited into a home down the street from the compound entrance for breakfast. We just said "Hi" to a woman and her son as they were eating breakfast on their screened veranda, which faced the street, and they invited us in. Our hostess was an older woman, and she and her son regaled us with stories of their life in Golfito while feeding us a wonderful meal of eggs, bacon and English muffins - what fun!

We spent the next two days just wandering around the town, and reading in our cabin. We sat on the screened-in veranda of our cabin and enjoyed the evening breezes when it rained. The jungle beyond the veranda was thick, noisy, and uninviting.

The day before the train was to leave we spent some time with the Mr. Block, "*el jefe*," manager of the Banana Company Compound and, on July 19, 1961, he gave us free Costa Rican Banana Company train passes from Golfito back to Puerto Gonzalez Vazquez where we had come from; and also passes on another train that would get us to the Panama border. His secretary gave us a loaf of bread which we ate with some "*piña dulce*," the jam Señora Alverado had sent along with us.

The morning we were to leave Golfito the water was a shiny blue, like the sky, and the lush green vegetation contrasted with it to create a sort of fairyland atmosphere in the morning quiet. It was cool in the house, but it got quite hot outside during the day.

CHAPTER 17 - PANAMA

"The only substitute for experience is being nineteen."
Author unknown

July 21, 1961 (six weeks since the start) Reaching the country of Panama itself was anticlimactic. The train simply reached a certain point along the track in the middle of miles of banana plantations and stopped. Then we were told to get off. That was around 2:00 p.m. and, after " crossing the border", which meant showing our passports to a fellow in a shack beside the railroad track in the middle of a bunch of a million or so banana trees. The train reversed direction back to Costa Rica, and we began walking down the railroad track in a southerly direction along with a dozen or so other Central Americans.

We got the impression that not too many *gringos* passed that way, and that gave us some pride. The other people seemed to know where they were going and they kept walking, so we did too. We discovered a French student among us who was also hitchhiking to see the world. He said he spoke French, German, Spanish, and English, and he was studying Japanese.

As we trekked, people would leave the tracks to pick bananas off fallen banana trees, so we did too. Among the endless miles of banana trees there were randomly fallen ones. The bananas off of those trees were within reach and were perfect.

We got stuffed on bananas; we stuffed our sacks with bananas - I have never seen such beautiful and delicious bananas before or since. It made all the uncertainty of our travel plans that much easier to bear. If nothing else, we could roll out our sleeping bags and eat fabulously delicious, perfected bananas for the rest of our lives. That would be good except that Fred kept reminding me of all the different types of horribly deadly poisonous snakes that we had been told about that love to live around banana trees. So, we picked up some bananas, but we also kept on walking.

Carl on a railroad bridge in Panama

A man in a tractor pulling a wagon came out of one of the rows of banana trees, so a bunch of us hopped on it. There were no objections, so it must have been alright. We had been walking half an hour or so by that point. We had no Panamanian money, so it was lucky no one asked us to pay for anything. I got into a chat with one of the banana plantation workers, and he suggested a railroad cut-off to follow if we were headed for David, Panama.

We took the suggested cut-off and shortly had to cross a bridge. Midway on the bridge a railroad bus (a pickup truck with the wheels converted to railroad wheels) came along from in back of us. The driver stopped and we told him of our goal to reach David. He told us he thought we were *muy loco*, very nuts, to be going to David from the railroad, but invited us to hop on so he could take us toward the Pan American Highway, which we could then take to David.

When it was time for us to go our separate ways, he told us to hop off and pointed in a certain direction. We were alone at that point in the middle of nowhere and neither of us knew just where to go. The only thing we could see in every direction were rows and rows of banana trees and different rail lines. We started down the track we thought we had been told to take.

Suddenly, as the track curved, more civilization appeared before us in the form of a railroad work crew and their little work crew-like flatbed railroad car. They were almost done for the day so a group of us stood around waiting to hitch a ride. As soon as the workers and their tools were all on-board, the rest of us all piled on their car and off we went through the jungle - what a sight! In my mind I can still see Fred, sitting across from me, hanging on to some piece of the machine and really getting into his Spanish with some of the other travelers - the wind blowing his hair all around and the jungle rolling by - that was a scene!

In fifteen minutes we arrived at a regular train station where we all piled off and began waiting for the real thing. The station was full of native banana plantation workers. These guys are pretty sturdy looking, and pretty deeply tanned. They didn't do much talking, but they sure did stare, all of them. If we could have melted from a stare, we would have been little puddles because every one of them had their eyes fixed on us - like, we had forgotten to put on our trousers or something. Anyway, they meant no harm, they were tired, and we were there, and they stared. In half an hour the train arrived.

You'd have thought this train was the train to heaven when it arrived - it was an unmitigated mob scene with everyone from the station attempting to climb on-board. It looked like an old time Lionel steam engine but in full life-size. Fred and I played it cool - we constantly had this concept of some great movie being made of our adventure and each step of the way we had to consider how our actions would come across on the big screen. We were the heroes here, the guys in the white hats. So, in keeping with our self-image, we waited until the last second to get on, just to be cool. We were cool. We were the only white guys, and even though these guys were tough looking, they were all very kind in any interaction we had with them.

The train took us to a little town near David. Fifty taxis were waiting at the station when the train pulled in, and we knew we were back in civilization again. The cabbies were grabbing people off the train to take to David, which was the biggest city in northern Panama. We didn't take any taxi, we just walked right by asking directions to the Pan American Highway.

We got to the highway shortly, and, after the regular sudden afternoon rainstorm drenched us, we managed to get our ponchos out of our bags. Seeing our plight, a passing taxi stopped and one of the passengers invited us to ride with him to David - and, who should it be but the French student we had left when we had crossed the border! He was now traveling with a young Panamanian and his new bride, who insisted we get in and paid our fare.

In David we went straight to the police station to line up a place to sleep. They greeted us there like old friends. They turned their library over to us as a dormitory. The inmates were free to walk around in the station, and one of them broke into some guy's concession stand and gave us all kinds of goodies to eat. It wasn't our fault; we never asked him to break into the thing. It was a pretty casual police station; we fit right in.

We spent the evening walking around town and talking with the policemen. They all thought we had a pretty good chance of catching a ride from David south to Panama City, so we decided to recommence our hitching the next morning. I slept that night on a cot and Fred slept on a big table. We got up at about four the next morning and walked to the outskirts of town.

At about 6:30 in the morning a local resident came up to us and told us that there was another road out of town and that there had already been all kinds of traffic on it this morning. He helped us get a ride over to the other road where we waited fewer than five minutes before getting a ride in a 1952 Jeep station wagon, just like the one my parents had back in San Diego.

We rode in the Jeep for about ten miles while the driver tried his English on us. He had worked in San Francisco about ten years before, and loved to speak English. Within five minutes of being dropped off, we were picked up

Pop's 1952 Jeep Station Wagon

by a road materials engineer working on a World Bank project. That ride was like dream. He took us half way to Panama City over the roughest part of the road to a point where the road to Panama City was all paved. We got out of his truck after some interesting talk about American foreign policy in Laos, Tom Dooley, etc. and began waiting in a town called Santiago.

Another jeep picked us up and took us south of Santiago about ten miles where we were picked up by the driver of a bread truck which had a door which opened to the wind and a broken latch.

We had to hold on for dear life to the inside of the door frame to keep the door from catching the wind and flying open. Four of us were stuffed in the front seat and we felt like we'd be thrown out if the door flew open.

When that truck let us off we got picked up by an old Panamanian man with three adults and five kids stuffed in an old Ford sedan. When we got in that car they arranged themselves so there were three adults and four kids all crunched in the back seat. Fred and I and the old man and our bags and one kid were in the front. The old Ford he had was always hitting bottom but he sure was a Godsend to us.

He left us off in a town called Aguadulce, where three black teenagers (two girls and a boy) picked us up and took us seven or eight more miles in the direction of Panama City.

Our next wait was another short one before a salesman who was going all the way to Panama City picked us up. He was just coming home from a weekend party, and he had family down in Panama City. I didn't all together understand what was going on, but he bought us some food that we appreciated, except for this delicacy which he wanted us to eat which looked like old gelatin and tasted like concentrated sugar. I still don't know what it was. I swallowed as much of it as I could getting all sticky as anything, and, since I was sitting in the back seat of the car, I could get away with throwing some of it out the window. Sometimes you have to thank people and just be as kind as you can without hurting their feelings when you don't like something that they treasure.

CHAPTER 18 - BALBOA, CANAL ZONE

> "Progress went on for a long time, then it went on too long."
>
> Ogden Nash

On July 24, 1961, we were dropped off in Balboa in the Canal Zone in front of a place called the Club House, where we could eat an American dinner. We asked at the Club where the local YMCA was so that we could get a room for the night. They told us that only Canal Zone residents and their guests could rent rooms in the Zone, and, since we weren't either, we couldn't.

We wandered into a Pentecostal church service to see if they had a place we could stay for the night, but they told us that they "were a little limited right now," even though they obviously had a huge, mostly empty building. With their 200,000 plus square feet of available floor space, Fred couldn't help but commenting that, yes, we understand, "Carl is a pretty big boy..."

After dinner we spent some time walking around the "Zone" before a police car drove up beside us to ask what we were doing. We enthusiastically told the police officer our story and he was very kind but he told us that it was a simple fact of life that we couldn't just sleep out in the park like we had done everywhere else. He told us that if we didn't have a place to stay in the Canal Zone, we couldn't *be* in the Canal Zone. He offered us a place to stay that we couldn't refuse: the Federal holding facility, in other words the jail, and we accepted his offer.

This Federal jail was awe-inspiring. We were treated just like any other inmates. Our bags were checked in for storage, we were given gray uniforms and led through several large, heavy steel clanging doors by big guys wearing guns. Our cell had two bunks and a ceiling of heavy steel mesh beyond which, in the morning, we could see reflected daylight. I wanted the top bunk because I had never had my own bunk bed; Fred slept below. We had a great night's sleep, but waking up in the morning was sobering - what if they decided not to let us out?

The alarm sounded and everyone got up at the same time in the morning. We had a few minutes to wash up and get ready for breakfast. Breakfast was coffee, oatmeal and toast and it was just like what you get at a restaurant. We sat and ate with the other inmates and got a lot of silent stares; we just didn't feel like talking. The guys there were not real friendly to us - I don't care what Johnny Cash says about prisons, these guys just didn't seem very friendly. I was glad to get out of that place.

When they let us out at about eight in the morning they told us that either we would have to have another place to stay that evening or we had to leave the Zone. We decided to split up to see if we would have any luck finding a place that way. We didn't want to leave the Zone because we wanted to try to get a job on a boat going back to the United States and we stood a much better chance of getting a job in the Zone than we would have in Panama City itself. Besides, it was a three or four mile walk from Panama City to anyplace in the Zone where we could have looked for a job.

The difference between the Canal Zone (Balboa) and Panama City (which was controlled by Panama just like any other part of the country), was like the difference between the American Compound and the little squalid town of Golfito. The Canal Zone felt like home to us. All the houses looked like regular American houses with American cars and American lawns, American roads with curbs and sidewalks, and American people. It felt so good to be back in a place that we didn't feel was contaminated all over the place; where we could drink the milk, eat the butter, and just relax and enjoy life again without feeling like our lives were constantly threatened by the water, food, and sometimes even the people.

I learned why people who have been away from home for years kiss the tarmac when they finally return to their familiar native land. Anyway, we felt great in the Zone and wanted to do everything we could to stay there.

We checked in at the port captain's office for jobs on ships, but there was nothing that we could be hired for. Then we went over to the Balboa Yacht Club to see about getting a job working on somebody's yacht. There we met an old man who had a yacht on dry dock who didn't know where he was going on his next journey, although he had been thinking about the Galapagos Islands. After that we went back to the Club House for lunch.

Fred and I agreed upon an evening meeting location and split up for the day to look for work and a sponsor. Fred returned to the yacht club and I headed for the port captain's office again. Along the way it began to rain and I stopped under a tree. While I was seeking shelter under this tree, a teenage boy walked by, and just for a chance, I told him our story. He told me to come over to his place because his folks might be able to help us.

The Reynolds were a wonderful family. Richard, Jr., whom I had met, had seven other brothers and sisters and their house looked just like my parents' house in San Diego.

What a joy to hear people speaking

The Reynolds' home in Balboa, Canal Zone, Panama

English everywhere and eating Corn Flakes and hot dogs just like we had always done. I retold my story to them and they directed their kids to make some adjustments in their sleeping arrangements so that I could have a bed. They were going to treat me as though I were just one of their kids who had been away for a while.

I told them about Fred and that we had planned on meeting at 5 PM down by the police station and they were just as concerned about Fred as they were about me. Just before 5 that evening Mr. Reynolds and I hopped into his truck and drove down to pick up Fred, who was already nervously waiting. Fred had gotten us a dollar-an-hour construction job offer, if we "could get the approval from the Panamanian officials" that we needed. That seemed like a very big long-shot.

We told the Reynolds how we had gotten to Panama and that we wanted to see the Canal. Fred told me later that when they talked about going to mass on Sunday they were surprised to learn that I was an atheist. Nevertheless, they didn't treat me any differently after I told them that.

The following day was a Sunday and all the shipping agencies were closed so we couldn't hunt for work. Mr. Reynolds, with his family of eight children, decided to take me and Fred sight seeing. They told us we could stay as long as we wanted - a week if necessary, and we told them we had to ship out by Tuesday at the latest to get back to school on time. They took us down to the newspaper offices to tell our story, and, on July 26, 1961, our hitchhiking trip was front page news - with a picture! - in the "Panama American" newspaper!

We checked General Delivery the next day and Fred had a letter from his Mom, and his girl friend, Sally. In his journal he wrote: "If I got any more letters I think I'd be homesick for sure." We were happy we got to Panama; we were ready to be back home, but that would be a couple more adventures off.

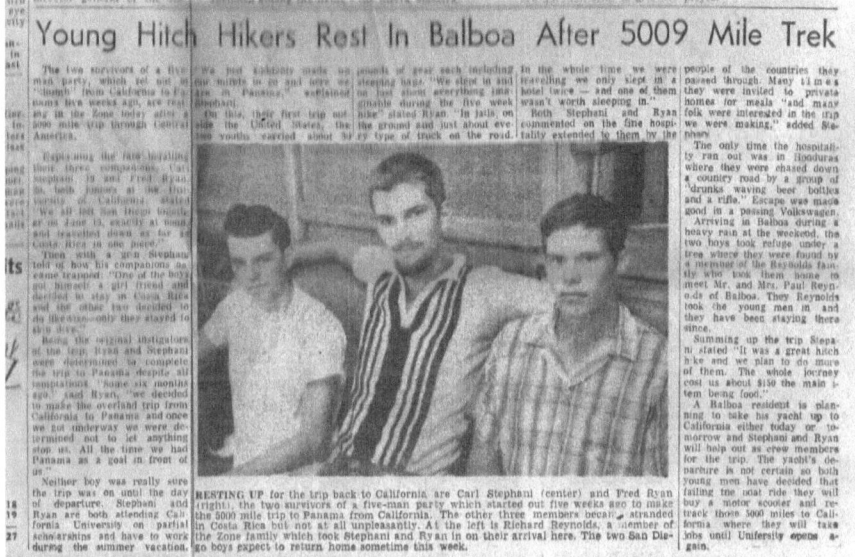

Front page of the Panama American newspaper below the fold July 26, 1961

Three days after we arrived, we hiked over to the Balboa (Canal Zone) Yacht Club to see if anyone was sailing out. We spent some more time talking with the fellow we had met earlier, William Kaul. He was a retired farmer from Cleveland, Ohio, who had just bought a 36' wooden ketch, the Qui Viva!, somewhere in the Caribbean to take to the Easter Islands. He had been a farmer all his life but he had always had a dream of buying a sailboat and just sailing his retired life away on the seven seas. He smoked little long skinny Marsh Wheeling cigars and looked like a short version of Ernest Hemingway.   Fred and I liked him and he seemed to like us.

That week we got to see some sights in Panama, including the Canal, which was, after all, supposed to be the whole point of THE TRIP!

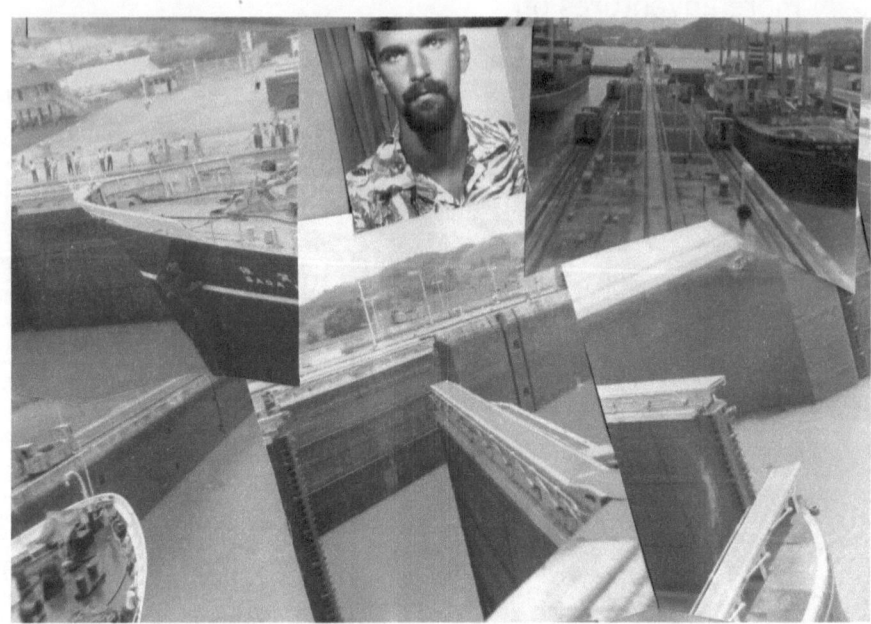

Canal photos - from a collage in Carl's scrapbook

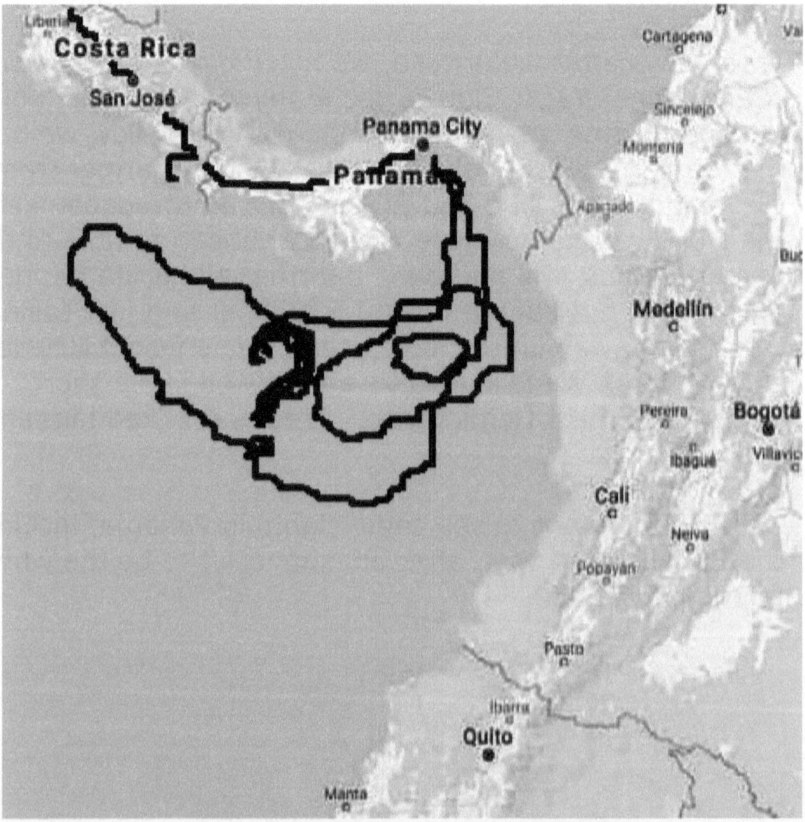

Possible course of the Qui Viva

Map data ©2018 Google, INEGI

CHAPTER 19 - QUI VIVA

"Never attribute to malice that which is adequately explained by stupidity."
Hanlon's Razor

The Qui Vival was not in terrific shape so Bill had it drydocked at the Yacht Club while he was having it caulked, painted and generally repaired. We got to talking with him and worked out a deal whereby we would help him get all his work done, and together we would sail to San Diego. We worked for the next three or four days full-time with him to get the boat ready.

We replaced nearly all the cable "stays" (otherwise known as "ropes," which hold the masts in a vertical position) on each of the masts because the original stays were either missing, broken, or frazzled. We also replaced most of the rigging and loaded what seemed like endless tons of ballast to stabilize the floating of the boat. We cleaned out the forward bunk compartment, and had the bilge pump and the fresh water tank pump repaired. Bill bought new mattresses and pillows for us, and that was nice.

Fred had bought a copy of Dr. Zhivago to read "while out at sea," and I had The Brothers Karamazov; although the captain told us we would have plenty to do just keeping the boat moving properly, sleeping, and making meals for ourselves.

July 26th was an anniversary for Fidel Castro's revolutionary movement and a lot of policemen were on alert in Balboa and in Panama City. A policeman visited the Reynolds house with some films of some activities he had been involved with earlier that week where he had two ribs broken by a stone-throwing mob. Mr. Reynolds had to go to Colon, or Cristobal, on the Atlantic end of the Canal, to report for duty.

Before Bill would actually let us set sail with him, he

required that we get permission slips from our parents. We each sent a wire to our parents, and they wired back that it was alright for us to go.

Bill actually wanted to sail to the Galapagos Islands, but he didn't have a crew and he didn't really want to go alone; so, in a way we were an unexpected blessing to him and he was happy to go to San Diego with us. He was also thinking of selling the boat and thought the market in San Diego might be good.

Fred and I thought that we might not be able to sail the entire way with him because it would take so much time. We thought we might have to get off at Mazatlan or Acapulco and hitch the rest of the way. Some of the people at the yacht club estimated that it could take us up to eight weeks to make it all the way to San Diego. Based on our limited knowledge, somehow we couldn't believe that could be true.

Neither Fred nor I had ever sailed a boat before, but we didn't think that mattered much. We both knew how to paint and tie ropes; and, although we didn't know any knots that had any regular names, we weren't afraid of anything - so there!

On July 29, the day before we were to leave the Reynolds home and begin living out of the boat, we went shopping. Bill Kaul, the old man, was quite a cheapskate. We figured the trip would take us about two weeks, so we pooled enough money between the three of us to buy food for more like two and a half or three weeks. Reynolds got us into a Canal Zone commissary so we saved some money that way. What a great family they were!

At the Tagaropulos, a local store on Avenida Cuba #26-38 we bought:
      1 case Monarch pork and beans
      ½ case Campbell's green pea soup
      ½ case Campbell's chicken noodle soup

    ½ case domino sugar
    20 lbs. of flour
    2 dozen eggs
    2 jars of green Amico olives
    2 tins of Lipton tea
    1½ cases of Monarch unsweetened grapefruit juice
    2 -12 ounce jars of Kraft red raspberry preserves
    2 - 12 ounce jars of Kraft strawberry preserves
    2 bottles of Maggi tomato catsup
    1 dozen boxes of vanilla pudding, and a dozen boxes of chocolate

That cost us $39.18; we split it exactly three ways.

The last day before we left we also bought a fire extinguisher and extra rigging (which we first inaccurately referred to as "rope") to take along just in case. Although we had gone in and out of Fort Amador several times before, when we picked up these last few things the guards decided we may be some kind of threat and really grilled us about what we were going to do with the stuff, and so forth. Ultimately the let us in for our last visit.

After lunch that day we all decided to take a nap. Captain Kaul went down into the cabin; Fred and I dozed on the deck where there was a cool breeze. When Fred woke up he said that for a moment he had no idea where he was. He could see jungle islands on one side and land on the other; then he realized he was in the Canal Zone, in the Republic of Panama, *muy lejos de mi casa* - very far from home. "It was really the strangest feeling."

The ketch had two rooms in it; a kitchen with a dining area across from the stove and ice box, and a forward bunk room. There was also a little closet for a toilet between the dining room and the forward cabin. The dining area made itself into a bed and that was where the "captain" kept his gear and slept. At the rear end of the boat on deck was the outside seating area, a square area about six feet on a side.

The Volvo engine was directly beneath the seating area and at the back of the seating area was the handle that controlled the rudder - the "tiller". Right in front of the tiller was a compass mounted on a post. There was a mast right in back of the seating area - the "mizzen" mast - with a sail on it. The main mast was forward of the captain's cabin, and, in addition to the main sail, it held the jib sail - a little sail that went out forward of the main sail and was attached to the long pole that stuck out in front of the boat.

An one point we almost picked up an additional crew member: Charlie Ford, another American wanderer. He offered to help us work on the boat, but then decided he'd rather fly back home to the United States.

Ross had written Fred at General Delivery in Balboa. Ross had planned to leave for California on July 25th or 26th, so he was well on his way home while we were working on the boat. Fred worried about Ross -"The dumb nut's probably married by now..."; I was still annoyed that he had given up on us and stayed in Costa Rica.

The Tuesday on which we were supposed to have left we were still in port waiting for our inboard auxiliary four cylinder Volvo engine to be fixed and for permission to buy 30 gallons of gasoline. The mechanic finally got the Volvo to turn over. We loaded all our stuff into the boat; the captain paid the bill at the Yacht Club; and they pushed the old Qui Viva! down the old ramp and into the water with us on-board! How exciting was that!!

On Wednesday, August 2, 1961, at about 1 PM Bill was at the rudder and we gave the old starter button the old push and before too long the old Volvo started coughing along and we were on our way! Chug-a-chug-chug we went out into the lane where we were allowed to go and off we went putt-putt-putt on a beautiful clear-blue-sky day with all our gear stowed away and the Reynolds' address in our address books so that we could write them when we got home.

Before we got going out to the open ocean we had to get gas. Bill had a very tricky maneuver to make to get us tied up to the yacht club dock to get our gas. The maneuver was too tricky for us and we ended up bumping into the yacht of the President of Panama! Ouch! Luckily no one was on-board so we just got our gas and headed out into the Canal traffic.

We were supposed to have a professional port pilot take us the first part of the way so that we wouldn't cause a delay to the international freight traffic going through the Canal, but we didn't have the money, so we just started off when we were ready. After we had gassed up, Fred took the rudder and got us safely out to sea - sufficient indication, as he said, "that no professional pilot was necessary."

Fred at the helm looking good!

You had to leave Balboa bay under power because with all the shipping going through the Canal they couldn't afford to have some crappy little sailboat tacking back and forth holding up a giant chunk of the world's shipping while it worked its way out of the bay. You had to get at least fifteen miles out from the Club docks before you could shut down your engine and start to sail.

It was a lovely day! Just plain beautifully lovely and exciting! The old man was smoking one of his Marsh-Wheelings and Fred was turning the rudder this way and that to keep us just on the right course. Really gigantic transport ships were in front and in back of us, we were on the sea and traveling and it was just pure fun! Open air, open sea, free men on a wild journey - chug-a-chug-chug our little Volvo engine kept plugging along and we were masters of our fate. I took some pictures with my Kodak because this was a time to remember!

About 90% out of the Bay our little Volvo suddenly stopped its chug-a-chugging. Captain knew we weren't out the legal distance yet but he gave the order to raise the sails anyway because we had no other choice. Fred and I flew into action and in minutes the main and mizzen sails were up and then we really were ON OUR WAY! That was the first time we had ever raised sails on a real sail boat in our lives.

Sailing is beautiful. There is no engine noise, no nothing - just the breezes and the squeaks and the splashes as the boat cuts its way. We were all elated. What freedom, what joy, what peace, and yet what excitement! Nothing but the ocean before us and the wind and sunshine at our backs! As we sailed along we began to wonder what had happened to the Volvo, and what it would take to get it started again. We checked the ballast around the engine compartment and all the caulking seemed to be holding just fine.

That afternoon when I had gotten up on the main mast to

arrange some rigging the wake from one of the ships hit us and I nearly got flung off. Fred shouted up at me, and I shouted back that "that was fun!"

Carl up on the main mast

We sailed all that afternoon in a southerly direction with the captain at the rudder and Fred and me learning how to coil and release the ropes without tangling them; how to tell when to let the boom out more to keep the sail full; and how to sit to properly to be able to manage the rudder. There was a lot to learn, but the captain was pretty patient with us and drew his knowledge from the experiences he had had sailing on the Great Lakes.

That afternoon we had lunch and when we had some free time we decided to check out the little Volvo to see what was up. We opened the engine compartment and cranked the engine over a few times to see if there was any spark, and, sure enough, she had spark and we knew the wires and the spark plugs were good because we had just put in new ones.

Next we pulled one of the plugs, as we had done several times when we had been in port to see what we could learn by looking into the cylinder. Cap'n gave the order to hit the starter button, ol' Volvo turned over once and then shot out a blast of water. That was not a good sign. Cap'n stuck his finger into the cylinder to see what kind of water it was, and, sure enough, salt water. We either had a crack in the block, or some other way, water was getting into the cylinders. Real sailors disdained the use of internal combustion engines anyway, cap'n told us, but we were a little disappointed that all the work we had done on the engine the past week had been for nought. On the other hand, at least it had gotten us out of the bay and that was really all that we absolutely needed.

*Carl at the helm
Captain Bill Kaul watching*

We closed up the engine

compartment, cooked up some dinner and assigned shifts for sailing through the night.

The stars came out that evening and wherever the boat hull created a splash or swirl the plankton lighted like millions of little neon-greenish stars in the water; as though the water were filled with sparks from a greenish-yellow fire.

The first night I saw the plankton luminesce I took a bucket with a rope on its handle and pulled buckets of water up to throw out on the ocean's surface. When the water from the bucket would hit the ocean's surface it would give off an explosion of light - it was just beautiful. We didn't go swimming the first day because we were just too busy putting everything in place, learning how to set the sail and how to tie knots with names.

The first night was a good one. We divided the night up into three two-hour shifts, and we each got an assignment. We didn't mind our two hour night watch, probably because we didn't know what potential dangers lurked out there for us in the middle of the Pacific Ocean. The job was simply to hold the tiller to keep some wind in the sails, and to keep the boat pointed in the direction of some star we would pick out that evening to aim for. Every so often we would check the compass with a flashlight to double check our bearings.

We had a radio-based direction finder and a nautical map in the cabin which we used about once a day to check our location. The direction finder was just a radio with an antenna that could be turned 360 degrees. The map showed the location of landside radio transmitters and by turning the antenna to tune into one of them we could tell what direction we were from that transmittter. Then we would check our location against another ground-side transmitter, and where the signal direction lines from those two ground-side transmitters crossed, there we were. Our first day we got out about fifty miles into the ocean, and we were pretty pleased.

The second day we got to a point about one hundred miles out of Panama City, about seventy miles off the coast - we were really sailing and Fred got really sea sick. I hated to see him vomiting overboard because it almost made me get sick too, but I guess he hated it even worse. Fred was in a state of minor sea sickness for the first three days. That helped save on our provisions.

The second afternoon we hit a lull in the wind so there wasn't much to do. The ocean was crystal clear blue as far as you could look down, there were no signs of civilization anywhere, just blue ocean and blue sky - and the cap'n was asleep below deck. Fred and I decided to have some fun so we stripped down to our underwear and into the drink we went. Fred jumped first, just off the side of the deck. He must have gone 12-15 feet down into the water, but the water was so clear you could see every wrinkle on his face as he went down. I jumped in right after him and we splashed around for a few minutes.

Captain Kaul on deck watching for sharks

Right in Panama City there was a lot of garbage in the water. Sharks infested those waters because there was so much food. Several times when we went into Panama City we went over to the docks to look at the ocean and we saw shark fins from the sharks circling around food that had been thrown in the water. The only swimming done along the coast anywhere close to the Canal was done at beaches that were fenced for sharks.

While we were swimming that day in the mid-ocean, a gorgeous vividly colored four foot long fish swam by us. It looked about ten times more colorful underwater than any fish I had ever seen - its colors had a neon-like glow as they reflected the sunlight underwater.

The cap'n heard us swimming and got up from his nap to come look around. He took a slow look scanning the horizon. We were only a few feet from the side of the boat, when all of a sudden he shouted "SHARKS!" Fred and I shifted into high gear and began swimming our little hearts out to get back on-board. I was out of the water in no more than thirty seconds, Fred was right behind me, and before he got both legs out of the water a shark at least ten feet long came cruising right beneath where we had climbed up the boarding ladder! WoW! That was scary. No more king of the oceans were we.

We went swimming almost every day from then on but with one of us watching and one swimming.

Carl on deck enjoying the view

CHAPTER 20 - THE STORMS

> "Behold the wonders of the mighty deep,
> Where crabs and lobsters learn to creep,
> And little fishes learn to swim,
> And clumsy sailors tumble in."
>
>   Anonymous

Our third day we were probably 150 miles or so out to sea and not making much headway. We talked about the Japanese current that goes southward toward the equator along the Central American coast and the need to get out beyond it to move north. Bill told us about the "doldrums" where the winds just stopped blowing and the boat just bobbed about in the ocean, more or less directionless.

The day began with the western skies blackened and we could sense that the black clouds were moving our way. We had hours to prepare, the winds picked up a little bit and we got moving along somewhat. For at least half a day we watched the black western sky get closer and closer to us. We talked about how to handle the rigging to avoid tangling when we let the sails down. We sailed and watched, and sailed and watched, and I didn't like sailing and watching; it was eerie.

Finally the clouds got close enough that we could see where the rain was hitting the ocean surface. Bill told us we would be able to hear the rain before it hit us, and we heard it, just like he said. We sat together around the tiller waiting as the wind began to pick up. Little droplets started falling all around our little boat. They reminded us of playing out in the summer rain when we were kids and everything different was fun.

For two or three minutes we savored the raindrops and then WHAMMMMMM!!! -seventy mile an hour winds hit us like the blast of a jet engine and our little boat was laid down sideways with the main sail in the water and the cap'n screaming "GETTT THAT SAIL IN!!!!!! GET THAT SAIL

IN!!! OR WE ARE DONE FOR!!! NOWWWWW!!!!!

Carl at the tiller in the rain

More than a hundred miles out in the middle of the Pacific Ocean, floating around on a bundle of rotten wood, half turned over with its sail in the water and the old man screaming death at us as loud as he could, this was not fun! There was no proper warning, there was no courtesy, there was no anticipation - just a few raindrops, then BLAST YOU!! and the ocean wants to take you down!!!

Rigging was flying everywhere and we pulled our hearts out trying to get the main sail pulled onto the deck. The deck was slick as ice and I wondered what happened if you slipped off??!! No room for mistakes for about four minutes of absolute hysteria, then we just went to work battening down everything and getting ourselves inside the cabin.

The wind roared and the rain poured for about four hours and our little boat bounced around like a cork for what seemed like an eternity. The forward cabin where Fred and I were bunked had enough room for two 18" wide bunks and an aisle - nothing more. We packed ourselves in there listening to the angry ocean beating against our little boat and hoping it would not break up and sink. We kept our eyes on the little square escape hatch above us over the center aisle, and wondered if we would have to use it.

One of the nice things about the Qui Viva, the cap'n had explained to us, was the fact that it had a "hurricane deck". That means that the deck was designed to offer the least amount of resistance to the wind because of its low cut design, and smooth corners. He also told us about the boats that each year are found floating around the oceans of the world without anyone on them because their one man crew got careless on deck and slipped off in the middle of one of these storms. Under those conditions, even if there were other crew members they would be pretty helpless to turn a boat around to find someone lost at sea. This sailing stuff began to take on a less rosy hue in our minds after this first storm, but at least it would be a cheap way back home?!

As soon as we had a chance to catch our breaths and understand the seriousness of our situation and actions, cap'n reminded us that we had better get our kerosene lanterns up on the deck lighted so that if we did come within crashing distance of another boat, at least they would have some chance of seeing us - Fred and I got the lanterns, lighted them and hung them on the wire stabilizers on each side of the main mast, red on the left, green on the right. Cap'n had safety ropes for us to use when we went up top and we clipped one end of the safety ropes to the cables that went around the deck and the other end to our belts - they were to help us in case we slipped.

The cap'n suggested we put out a "rope anchor" to slow our drift somewhat. We had about 200 feet of 2 inch rope stowed aboard so in the pitch dark of the rainy night we went up top and slowly let the rope out until it was dragging behind us and tied on to the mizzen mast.

When the storm passed in the middle of the night we climbed up on deck to assess the damage. Half of the mizzen mast rigging had snapped as had a lot of the other rigging. Fortunately we had bought extra rigging. We made assignments for the night shift and continued sailing through the night.

The reality of the storm sobered us up firmly and the night shift became a trial of nerves whenever the sky was overcast - making us wonder when the next storm would hit. We practiced latching ourselves to the cables along either side of the deck so that if we ever did slip, something would keep us with the boat. We got a lot more serious about being sailors and began to feel less like wild adventurers and more like a couple of scared kids. The cap'n reassured us and checked our location. We were about 200 miles straight west of Balboa in the middle of ocean; hardly an inch north of where we had been when we left, although we might be out far enough to avoid the current that kept pulling us south.

Fred on deck waiting for a storm

The day after our first big storm we hit a dead wind in the middle of the day for a while. We tried fishing by dragging a line with a gigantic aluminum lure with a hook over the transom. We dragged that lure for days but never had any indication that anything was the least bit interested in it.

During the course of any particular day we would be joined by a group of porpoises that would come up beside our boat, play around for an hour or two and then take off into the distance.

Some of these days were beautiful. In the next few days we changed virtually all the rigging on the boat, swam almost every day, and the only thing that worried Fred and me was that we might never see land again. It got so that all I wanted was to get home so I could see my own family again, get in my own bed, and not have to be continually on-call for duty against some hellacious storm. I began to despair a bit of getting back in time for school and to hope that at least I wouldn't miss our family's fall hunting trip.

Fred suggested turning back to Panama after we had been out for about ten days and we were about 200 miles out in the ocean, but Bill said that the only place we could go now would be Costa Rica and who knows how long it would take us to get there. In addition, the coast of Costa Rica was mostly mangrove jungles at that point and we could have a lot of trouble finding a place to land. We decided to continue to struggle northwestward to California. Here are some notes Fred made on Friday, August 4 about our first few days at sea:

> At night and partially during the day we take watches of 2-on and 4-off. It's not bad. I really got sleepy last night, though. I was counting the seconds until the end of my watch. There is little moon so the night travel is rather dangerous, or it takes some thought anyway. The guy at the helm at night usually navigates by the stars and checks with the compass. It seems strange sitting all by your lonesome in the middle of the sea in the dark and quiet. I used to think light houses were relics of the past, but now - wow! - we would probably be piled up on some rocks already if they weren't around. We see ship's lights only once in a while.
>
> Carl and I went for a swim-bath yesterday. It was so cool

and refreshing. We were only out of the water about 30 seconds when a 6 foot shark appeared. We quit swimming for a while.

Yesterday for about an hour a school of porpoises swam along with us. They just swam along and didn't say a thing...

So here we sit, going nowhere but up and down, and that considerably ...

Funny thing, we had to sail almost south and even southeast sometimes at first. That seemed rather odd considering that we're going to California from Panama.

CHAPTER 21 - TURTLES AND FISH

"News of my death is greatly exaggerated."
Mark Twain

While we were sailing during the day, really huge sea turtles would start looking at us somewhere between one and two hundred feet away from the boat, and they would sometimes range in even closer. They would poke their heads up alongside the boat and look around for minutes at a time. These turtles had shells three to four feet across, and a head about as big as a volleyball.

The Captain told us that when he bought the boat in the Caribbean he had watched the locals catch turtles by swimming up behind them, clutching them around the neck with their thumbs jammed between their skulls and shells, and then turning their heads up so that they couldn't see where they were going. The turtles would then just swim as hard as they could but the swimmer on their backs would determine their direction.

The poor turtles would swim right up to the fishermen's boats onto which they would be promptly hauled aboard and prepared for dinner. I thought that sounded like a pretty exciting thing to do, so after a few days of watching and wondering, I decided to hop in the water to see if I could master the fine art of giant sea turtle catching.

I carefully swam out to get in back of the next one we saw and worked my way up to the back of his shell, and then grabbed. That turtle pulled his head in like a shot and I was immediately alone just out in the water splashing around. Several hours later we spotted another and I took a second shot; still no luck. We were beginning to think we would be sailing for quite a while, so it began to seem like a good idea to catch one of these turtles, if nothing more than to augment our dwindling food supply.

I tackled another one by jabbing my thumbs with lightening

speed behind his head and was able to prevent him from pulling his head back into his shell. Then, with my fingers wrapped around his throat and underneath his jaw, I turned his head upward and away we went. If I held his head up too high, his front flippers would come out of the water and we would go nowhere; but if I let him down a bit he would paddle and paddle and by kicking my feet in the water I could control exactly where he went.

I made him paddle over to the boat with Fred and the cap'n cheering me on, shouting and waving, until I got close to the boat; then they realized they had to do something. They leaned over the gunwale trying to sling a rope around it or something. By that time the captain noticed a shark in the water and it was time for me to get out. I let go of the turtle and they quickly pulled me aboard.

Then the next morning we spotted another one. It was a bit blustery and there were some waves breaking here and there, but there wasn't any storm on the horizon so it seemed alright to take a shot at it.

I leaped into the water and started heading toward him. This time the turtle seemed to sense our interest in him, and kept a bit of a distance between us. I persisted and eventually got somewhat close to him, but the waves were getting a bit stronger every minute.

As the moments passed, Fred and the captain began to feel the thrill of the chase a bit too, so to help me out they decided to put our little six-foot dinghy into the water and send Fred out to back me up.

The oars for the dinghy had gone overboard in a storm, so he had to use one of the flat one-by-ten inch seat planks to paddle. By the time they got the dinghy in the water and Fred maneuvered himself into it, the turtle was nearly 150 feet away from the boat and not getting closer. That didn't seem to be a problem because with the dinghy it seemed like there would always be a way to get away from the sharks, and to float around until we could rendezvous with the big boat.

As Fred got close to the turtle, I moved around to the turtle's back and began my attack routine. I grabbed his head and pointed him over to the dinghy. Then, when we got to the dinghy, I lined him up alongside it. Fred reached over and grabbed the side of his shell and pulled. The dinghy was about four inches above the water and had sides about ten inches tall. As we both pushed on the outside of the turtle, we got it sideways as though it were a flat dish with its back up against the side of the dinghy. Then we both shoved and managed to push and spin the turtle into the dinghy on its back with its head facing the rear. I hopped in the back of the dinghy because by now the wind was picking up some more and we were more than half a football field away from the boat.

The minutes spent paddling the dinghy over to the ketch were some of the most anxious of my life. A turtle's head is of a very simple design: a large bony rounded forehead with two small eyes and a small snout with an equally large rounded jaw on the bottom to meet it. A turtle's jaw just about allows the entire head to open in half, making it a huge, powerful pincer. The turtle was facing my end of the dinghy; my knees were on either side of the turtle on the bottom of the dinghy as I paddled. I had this great reluctance in my mind to continue in the position that I was in, but I didn't want to give up the turtle. I mentioned my predicament to Fred, who turned around, laughed, and just kept on paddling.

After five or ten minutes of paddling we got the dinghy over to the sailboat, which by now was listing to one side and the other in a great rocking motion because of the six-foot waves that were pushing it. As the gunwale came down on our side, Fred grabbed it. It steadily and firmly started its rise as Fred hung on and we got pulled up against the hull while his arm was stretched out and the boat rolled to the opposite side. Then the sailboat began its roll back to our side and under water we went - dinghy, turtle, me and Fred altogether. We were under the water trying to figure out what to try to save as the giant turtle swam happily away and the sailboat rolled back onto its other side again.

My first reaction was to try to save the dinghy; poor Fred was treading water as fast as he could just to stay afloat. I tried to get the plank paddles and the lead rope up to the captain. The dinghy was barely floating just below the surface of the water and I wasn't able to move it at all. Meanwhile I had wasted a minute or two and the wind kept carrying the sailboat away from us. Bill recognized our plight, forgot about the dinghy, grabbed a lifesaver ring, and started shouting "Swim! Swim! Swim for your life!" so we began swimming.

By that time Fred and I were fifty or sixty feet from the sailboat and we were losing on it fast. The wind was picking up and there were white-caps on the waves now all over the place. Fred was not all that good a swimmer, and, after the exhaustion of paddling so much, about all he could do was a little more than a dog paddle. The old man threw out the life ring and Fred grabbed it to get himself in. I just kept swimming trying to keep up with them.

By the time Fred got into the sailboat I was surrounded by white caps and I could only see the main mast of the boat in-between big waves. On any other day, we would have been surrounded by sharks in half the time, but either the white-water kept them away or they just didn't happen to be out that day.

On-board Fred was pleading with the captain to circle the boat around, but the wind was too strong and they couldn't tack back towards me. They threw out the life-ring for me the maximum one hundred feet, and I kept swimming. They managed to hold their own sailing against the wind for about fifteen minutes as I slowly closed in on the ring. I thought about nothing while I was swimming but when they finally pulled me aboard the boat, I couldn't believe what we had just done. My life had been held in the balance with that little swim in the ocean; there was no way to sail that boat into the wind, and it was pure luck that no sharks had come into the area. What a crazy thing to do, but it was done and it was over; the next thing to do was to survive the rest of the trip. Here are some of Fred's notes on those events:

August 7 Monday
Well, we're sailing along but making practically no real headway. I think we're still not far from Cape Mala. We went swimming today and even more quickly got some sharks.

I think it was Saturday we tried to catch another turtle. Carl swam quite far from the boat to get him but he couldn't get the turtle to swim back to the boat like he was supposed to. So I went out in the dinghy to help.

We managed to get the turtle in the dinghy but right on top of one of the oars so Carl couldn't use it to paddle. So I had to do all the work - and WORK it was! Finally I decided I couldn't make it by myself (the sea was rough with heavy swells) and after a little work I managed to free the oar. Then I was sitting on the turtle's back and Carl was kneeling and we headed for the boat.

With the Qui Viva rolling considerably, and us thus misjudging the tricky maneuver to get the dinghy in place next to it, Capt Bill with total disgust exclaimed "Oh, you hams!" as under we went. When we first went under and everything in the dinghy started floating away, I tried to retrieve a bunch of stuff, but then after gathering a couple of things, I looked over at the boat and was shocked to see the wind had blown it far away from us. I immediately forgot about retrieving anything, and started swimming for the boat through increasingly choppy water. I was almost exhausted by the time we had gotten the dinghy with the turtle up to the boat, and I very soon became totally fatigued. I had closed maybe half the distance to the boat, but there does come a point where a body pushed beyond its physical limits just doesn't obey the mind's commands, and I was having increasing difficulty just raising my arms to take forward strokes, and thus I was having trouble keeping my face above the water.

At this point I had that strange but not unknown sensation of looking down from afar at my plight, as at another person. Then, I was also somewhat surprised at the realization that, hmm, I'm not panicking (a welcome effect of my faith?).

There also was at this point a fragmentary but vivid awareness that every human tie, every human thought, emotion, hope for the future on this earth was seconds from being irretrievably extinguished forever. At this point Bill, apparently seeing our distress, managed to throw me a life preserver. I don't know how he managed a very long, and exceptionally accurate throw, splashing down only 2 feet from me. It's a monumental understatement to say that putting an exhausted arm thru that life preserver was an exhilarating feeling, and all those soon to be lost human attributes were dramatically resurrected again.

I don't know if ever in my whole life there has been a more powerful sense of relief as when my arm went into that life preserver, but maybe incongruously I did also have a momentary sense of regret for that turtle ....

Until I was out of the water, I didn't realize that Carl was also in serious danger, because he was always a much stronger swimmer than I was. It has always seemed a little poignant that both of us could have easily met our end, very close but far enough apart that we each fought our existential battle without the help of the other.

For some reason that day, no sharks had shown up.

We've each been taking 2-on and 4-off watches at night. It's working OK, I guess. The problem seems to be that we aren't making enough headway to get back to school in time. Oh well, we'll see what happens.

We had a monster storm yesterday. Bill said the winds were 70 miles per hour. Did we ever struggle with those sails, getting them down!

Every day before we stopped to take a swim, we got chased out of the water within five minutes by a shark or two. With that turtle I was in the water for 15 or 20 minutes. If the ocean hadn't been so rough, we likely would have been half digested by some shark by then, and there would have been nothing Bill could have done to prevent it. I realized how easy it would be to mis-calculate the ocean and end everything right there in the middle of nowhere.

Four big storms hit us during the first two weeks. The first one had come during the day, the second came in differently. About 2 AM one morning when I was in a deep sleep, like only you can get into by being rocked for hours and hours and hours and days and days and days until you are so tired you close your eyes until you hear an old man scream at the top of his lungs "CARL!!!!!! FRED!!!!!!!!!!! UP HERE!!!! UP!!! NOW!!!" And you feel the wind blowing and the boat rolling and the rain pouring and the captain yelling his orders and you are sound asleep but running and pulling and untying and hauling and wondering if all this fun is ever going to stop and you begin to wish it were all over and you tell the captain that you want to flag down the next ship that goes by so that you can get on it and he says that he will not let you get off the boat because you are his ticket to survival and alone he is dead but you don't care except that you know he has a little gun because you saw it when he took it out of his little locked closet one day to clean it and you know that if you jumped off this little sailboat he would not think twice about using it on your back so you talk about pulling close to land to be let off to swim ashore and the same comments are exchanged and you really begin to wonder if you are going to die on a sailboat off the shore of Panama with a crazy old farmer from Cleveland, Ohio.

We saw freighters way off in the extreme distance every day or two; we hadn't seen land in days.

Fred and I began talking about turning back; Bill would have none of that. He told us he would rather set the boat on fire than to turn back. We began to get on each other's nerves a bit. Here's what Fred wrote about those days:

> August 9 Wednesday
> We're still sailing along making about no headway. Many times we've lost at night what we had gained during the day, or visa versa, because the wind would die down. So, after the first couple of days of blasted stormy, scary wind and rain, we now get first gratefully received and now despised hot sun and no breeze. Since we spent the first week without getting around Cape Mala, which would allow us to turn northwest toward California, I asked Bill to head back to Panama (it would take 2 days, and we could start hitching or fly, or something). The way it was, we don't know when in the 20th Century we'll get back. However, Bill wouldn't have it. I think he'd be too embarrassed to go back. He

sees it as some sort of personal failure if the wind doesn't blow. The laughing he anticipates he would get at the yacht club couldn't be taken, he told us.

Anyway, Carl and I will get off at Puntarenas, Costa Rica, and not Mazatlan. Two days ago Bill said it would take a week to get there, and since then we haven't made 10 miles. So, I guess the only thing to do is grin and bear it. About two days ago I was so ready to get off this boat I would have gotten off at any point of land we saw. Trouble is, we haven't seen any land for about five days now. We are in a ship's lane still, so we see ships, freighters, every once in a while.

We had the motor and the sails going for a little while yesterday, but the worthless thing overheated again and we used a bunch of our fresh water to keep it cool because it had a bad radiator leak. We can't afford much more of that. Last night we hauled in sail (no wind) and hit the sack, checking every once in a while.

Well, about 1 AM Bill got us up (there was a tiny breeze) and we started to put up the sail. Carl was, I guess, a little doubtful about our chances of catching any breeze, and also was still sleepy. Anyway, he came up on deck, as Bill wanted, but was pulling to lift the main sail rather heartlessly. Bill noticed it and uttered a few angry curses, saying that if we didn't want to put up the f...ing sail, we didn't have to. So we all went back to bed. I think Bill was actually just looking for an excuse to get himself out of the position he had gotten himself into by calling us up to raise the sails in such a windless night.

Later that night, about 4 AM, Bill woke me up and said let's put up the sail. I got Carl, or so I thought, and went up on deck; however, Carl didn't show up. Bill blew his cork, went storming and yelling for lazy Carl to get up and not to try to pull that sort of stunt again, and he commanded that henceforth Carl would eat alone, wash his dishes alone, and do everything alone - and he topped that by calling him a lazy black bas.....d!

So, although the Pacific is tranquil now, we have not always had domestic tranquility aboard the boat. I think the main problem now is that whereas Bill is in the midst of an around-the-world loop, is retired and has nothing to do but sail till he dies, we have other things to do which are more important to us than sitting in this boat going sixty miles in eight days, and getting tongue-lashings at every turn. He thinks, however, that it must be the work, night watches, etc., which make us want to get off early. Oh well, neither of us is going to tell him anything anymore.

Today we snapped some rigging and spent all morning fixing it, plus we fixed a short in our short wave radio. There was no wind so it didn't matter anyway. Bill seems to enjoy repairing things. It is his idea of adventure and matching wits with the sea and nature, etcetera. Maybe if I were sixty-two I'd want to sit in a boat and do that, too - although now I can think of other things I'd like to do better. Right now, on this boat, I am ten times more anxious to get home than ever before. I would really like to be back in good ole California. Mostly it is this uncertainty which is bothersome. That is, if we knew we were making headway and that in a week we'd be in Puntarenas, it wouldn't be too bad. But we haven't the slightest idea when the doldrums will quit giving us the run-around, or when we'll hit Costa Rica.

The scene isn't all black, though. Today after fixing some more of the rigging - Carl went up on the cross-tree and swung like Tarzan up there with these ever present swells - we all stripped (we do that quite often) and went for a swim. It was magnificent and refreshing. This water is so cooling, and so blue and clear! I've never seen anything to match it. Even water in pools isn't so clear. We see, too, tiny fish just swimming around, not paying attention to anybody. Probably they had never seen humans before. I guess either they, or we, are pretty lucky... The boat looks really odd from the bottom. It's hard to describe. I think part of it is that it is so easily seen in such detail and in such clear water that one's thoughts, or only in a bathtub, or something like that, could such a sight be seen.

We tried today to catch some fish but we couldn't. A beautiful bluish-greenish-yellowish dolphin struck our line, but we didn't hook it. It was about 2-3 feet long. Some other 9"-12" fish swam around the boat today for a long time but we couldn't catch any of them either.

We finally saw the water snake that Carl had seen, but Bill and I hadn't. It looks exactly like any old water snake and just slithered along on top of the water. I imagine it's some kind of eel; but it looks just like a snake.

We're making about 3-4 knots an hour which actually is tremendous compared to what we have been doing. If we could average that much all the time I'd be tickled pink. However, that's too much to hope for. Good old Puntarenas is still at least 500 miles away.

If we ever get to Puntarenas before September we'll probably go see Noemi again and then go back to Señor

Cordova's house ... and then hitch to Juarez, Laredo, or Mexicali, and then hitch across the states. It sure is one giant trip, though. If we take the train through Mexico (they are very cheap) I'm almost positive we'll go first instead of second class. The memory of the train ride still hangs on bitterly.

About all I can say about our cruise is ... I sure never thought I'd ever be caught in the doldrums for days in a sailing ship.

We noticed that although we were far out to sea, we were in waters with dangerous underwater shoals all around us coming up practically to the surface and threatening disaster. As we had poured over Bill's charts, we learned they were sadly out of date and inaccurate. My thoughts about his lack of preparedness putting all of us in serious danger were not terribly kind at that moment. Bill had me climb out to the extreme end of the bowsprit so I could see more clearly where the most threatening ones were, and so I kept calling out Port! Starboard! trying to keep us clear of their jagged edges. Soon it became too dark to see because another monster storm was coming up, so all we could do was batten down the hatches and go below. The storm that night tossed us about as we slept very uneasily and with our life jackets on. How in the storm we missed those jagged rocks I had seen all around us seems like a miracle to me.

Finally, on August 10th, at the 4 AM change of shift Bill agreed to give up and head back to Panama. We had traveled west but not gone north at all so we pointed ourselves back toward land. On the horizon about every three or four days we had seen a boat pass by.

After a day of dedicated heading back to land, we were hit

by another storm. We didn't know if we were in a shipping lane or not and we just hoped that we wouldn't be blown into some giant cargo ship's path. To slow our travel in the wind, we let out our "rope anchor" again. During the daytime we were occasionally surrounded by little flying fish that shot across the boat like bolts from a crossbow. These little guys would shoot out of the side of a big wave when it would rise and they would sail for a hundred yards.

Groups of porpoises would follow us and then lead us with their backs rising out of the water as they dove and jumped.

The storms were incredibly frightening but our water supply was getting low after two weeks. The next time we were hit we set up a bucket brigade to catch the water that was caught on the main sail boom in a bucket. By this time we were really getting concerned about our survival. Even when we were surrounded all about by pitch black skies, broken by tremendous blasts of thunder and lightening, we would continue to try to catch the water in buckets and pour it into our fresh water tank.

Some time after two weeks the captain had some trouble with the stove when he was cooking pancakes for breakfast. He fiddled around with the valves on the white-gas stove and got it to work for the time being. After breakfast, just in case, he pulled the fire extinguisher we had bought out of its rack and as the three of us sat around watching, he broke the safety wire lock and pressed the button to spray some of the contents. Great, Worked fine. Three squirts. Valve stuck, continues to spray. Cap'n jiggles handle, bangs handle, pulls handle, shakes extinguisher - we all watch - pressure gauge on the extinguisher just keeps going down and down. We all try. The valve is stuck. The fire extinguisher is empty. What happens when you have a fire on a wooden boat a hundred miles out in the ocean? Well, you'd better get the fire out because if your boat burns up you don't have much left to work with, and we had already lost the dinghy.

That afternoon was a beautiful one. The sun was shining and the captain and I were sitting at the tiller just enjoying the day. Fred was in charge of cooking Campbell's soup and canned ham for lunch when he called out, "Cap'n, I need some help here!" I kept the tiller, and the captain went down the six steps into the cabin to see what Fred needed. Two seconds later he popped up out of the cabin with one hand on one end of the stove followed by Fred carrying the other end. The stove was completely engulfed in flames and it went immediately over the side without a word being spoken.

Fred and the captain sat down on either side of me. It was an hour or so before anyone spoke. We had to be thankful the boat didn't catch fire. We ate the sliced ham cold and mixed a can of soup with cold water for dinner. After a short conversation we all agreed we would do whatever it took to get ourselves back to Panama alive.

> August 10 Thursday
> Well, hip, hip, hurray! Last night at about 4 AM Bill informed us that we are heading back to Panama. That was the greatest kind of news possible. I never thought he'd do it.
>
> This morning Carl and I were sleeping on deck ... and we spotted land! It was really nice to see and reassuring in some strange way. Seeing the land made it seem as if maybe we weren't the only ones left in the world, after all.
>
> So now we're breezing along fairly well, along the Peninsula that Mala Point is on. We should make 60 miles today. That's almost as far as the actual distance gained from Panama in the last eight or nine days! Actually this morning we had, I think, about a hundred miles to go.
>
> The land that we spotted this morning was the same view

we had almost six whole days and several hours earlier. It was rather odd to see how little distance we had covered in all that time out at sea and all that work. But soon we should (soon, meaning 3-4 hours if the wind holds up) be able to cut north and head straight for dear old Panama. Bill figures we'll make it tomorrow afternoon some time.

Today we ran the engine for about 4 hours and used 5 gallons of our fresh water for the cooling system. Earlier when we had tried we had stopped after half an hour. By continually adding water we could have run it longer but something else also went wrong. We found water traces in the oil, which itself was sludgy as mud. Now the oil's drained and refilled with new oil, so with more water we should be set in case the wind dies. But Bill doesn't want to use the engine until we get almost there if we don't have to. I think he is anticipating feeling a little embarrassment at returning, judging from his comments - like trying to find another moorage.

This little cruise of ours is probably going to wind up costing us $25 and almost three weeks of time - wow! We'll have some groceries left which we'll try to re-sell, if Bill doesn't want them, which he probably won't. He is going, it seems, back to the States, too.

Our feelings about the whole thing are quite mixed. Right now, one day out and a good wind, it seems like the life of Riley. However, after having gone nowhere for days and days, and being blown around like leaves in a whirlwind, I could think of nothing I would rather not do. Now, though, the uncertainty and danger is almost vanished and things seem peachy keen. Maybe I should rack these days up as a lesson in patience. It sure took all I had, and probably more.

Carl wants to fly back to Miami and hitch across the States. I would like to also, if the price is not prohibitive. If I fly to Miami I'll get there with almost all of my dinero gone, but I had figured on that anyway and maybe it would be worth it to wrap up this trip quicker. I still might also hitch up the east coast and go to Detroit. It would be great to see things there again. It's been over 7 years since I left there.

Thinking about getting back has made me somewhat anxious for school to start. Getting a place to live should be interesting too. And that reminds me of darn old Ross. I haven't the slightest idea where he is now - he could be back in San Diego by now for all I know.

We'll probably eat ham tonight since this should be our last meal on-board - I hope! It is going to seem odd when we get on land again not to be flouncing, swaying, rocking and rolling back and forth, up and down, sideways and every other way. It's rather nerve-wracking sometimes when the plates, cups and silverware keep flying all over the place. Carl and I both want to leave Panama as soon as possible. We may go to the Reynolds' place, although I'm not sure. It may look a little bad if we just walk in and ask for a shower and maybe a bed and then just say goodbye and take off. I'm sure they would put us up, but there are certain social customs which seem to always work to louse things up.

August 11 Friday
They say one isn't supposed to count one's chickens before they hatch. Right now that sounds like pretty fair advice. Because, whereas yesterday we figured to be pulling in at about this time, now we figure we're at least a day out. Just

minutes ago I thought I sighted a trace of land again. If not, we probably don't know how far out we are. The sight of that land, which should be Cape Mala, perked our spirits up a bit. All three of us are getting tired of being battered around out here. Last night we really had a storm. Bill even flashed S-O-S signals to a passing freighter which, apparently, didn't see them. He was going to let us get off and then stay with the boat himself. I think, though, that we racked up some points with him by not pushing him to let us get off.

We just had a monster storm. Bill mentioned that it was almost hurricane velocity with rain like I've never seen before. We were so soaked it couldn't have been worse if we had been thrown in the ocean itself! The rain was welcome to some degree because we needed more fresh water to use in the engine cooling system. We gathered the rain in all the buckets we had. Because Bill wanted the water he kept delaying the order to haul down the main sail, even though the winds were becoming dangerously heavy. Carl and I kept looking at each other, and then at Bill waiting to be given the word to haul in the mainsail. But he just kept working to collect water.

Finally he yelled for us to take it in. We dashed to the ropes. The main is always a problem because it's so big and therefore catches a lot of wind. Because it catches so much wind it is particularly dangerous, especially in high winds. Once before we almost tipped the boat over because we hadn't gotten it in soon enough. And when we wait too long, like this time, the wind holds the sail tight against the mast so it won't come down of its own weight. So we hang and pull furiously in the pounding rain and screaming wind, all the time trying to keep from slipping overboard while the boat is rocking and lurching, rolling, and bucking.

In spite of the wind and rain, we managed once again to finally get the main sail down without damaging anything, except that because we ignored the mizzen mast so long, the mast shroud slipped and the mizzen mast nearly broke off. Bill was just about ready to chop it down. Before he did, Carl and I managed to get a makeshift shroud taker-upper made, and we saved the mast.

So we continue to sail along. I really hope we make it to shore one of these days. Now the sun's shining in a partly overcast sky with a brisk breeze - pretty good sailing although the waves are very choppy. Some day I hope again to see terra firma...

I'm writing this on the deck getting splashed by the cooling, worthless salt spray. Bah! The life of a sailor is fine for sailors, but I fear I am not one. At least not when my life is in danger ten times a day out in the middle of nowhere.

August 13 Sunday
Oh, brother! What a screwed up mess this is! After that last storm we sailed a while toward what we thought was Cape Mala. But, another storm, the worst yet, hit us again! It was really a bad one with terrific wind and pounding waves. It came at about 3 AM while I was at the helm. It had been clouding over for about three-quarters of an hour before, and the wind had already been quite brisk. I had a very hard time telling whether a storm was coming or not. Finally I decided to risk shouting wolf and I got Bill and Carl up on deck about thirty seconds before it hit! And hit it did - and wow!!

Again we hauled in the sail in howling winds and driving rain with the boat lurching all over the place. Again we were so soaked that we wrung buckets of water out of our clothes. I sincerely don't like that kind of sailing. If one of us had slipped overboard, there would have been absolutely no way we would have even had a ghost of a chance to be found.

So, that storm drove us probably a hundred miles away and we decided to head east and at this moment we are rolling well along either off the coast of Panama or Colombia. We haven't seen any signs of life and our short wave radio isn't picking up any signals, so we have no idea where on earth we are. We'll probably head south since we can't seem to go north with the wind always from that direction, and we'll try to see if we can find a coastal village or settlement of some kind. I sure hope we do. I'm just about totally disenchanted with our jolly little cruise.

A problem is that another of these blasted storms may come and push us way out to sea into the doldrums again. I would rather pack some food and try it overland than head out to sea again.

If this is Colombia we might have some trouble because we don't have visas for it. If it is, I hope the authorities are reasonable - I just now came across a Bible verse that had meant something to Linda, Ross's steady in California. Although our current situation puts it in a different context, it has seemed very refreshing to me. It's Psalm 56:13 - "For thou has delivered my soul from death; wilt not Thou deliver my feet from falling that I may walk before God in the light of the living?"

There was another item that gave me encouragement during

those days when it seemed we might never see land again. Our girlfriends, Linda and Sally, were quite faithful in writing letters to us, sending them to General Delivery in towns where we were expected to go. Some of Sally's and my correspondence has been kept as kind of a keepsake to this day. It happened that I picked up mail from both of them in Panama City, and I carried a letter from Linda intending to give it to Ross whenever I might see him next. Linda also became a close and valued friend of mine, and has been such all these years.

One night when we were all huddled below, being beaten about by yet another violent storm, I was feeling pretty discouraged at ever getting home, and I kept thinking of that letter to Ross for Linda, knowing that it would for sure contain words and thoughts of encouragement, but that sadly Ross would probably never see it since it would likely go down with us and the battered Qui Viva. A few days earlier in a similar scene, I had wrestled painfully with the idea of opening it and reading it, but my conscience wouldn't let me. This time, however, I was seeing two possibilities if I opened it: 1) we go down, and neither Linda nor Ross ever know that I read it, but I would get some emotional support from it in my last hours, or 2) we do in fact get back, and I have to confess to Ross and Linda, my very close friends, that I read their personal correspondence. Number 2 won. And I did receive encouragement and refreshing just from reading the kindly and happy way Linda related items of her life that summer. And I was forgiven.

CHAPTER 22 - RETURNING

> "I have met triumph and disaster, and have tried to treat those two impostors just the same."
>
> Rudyard Kipling

Seventeen days and four major serious storms since our initial departure we were fifty miles off to the southwest of Panama. We could see land all day. During the day a whale came up alongside us. We first noticed it as the ocean next to our boat became totally mirror calm for an area about thirty feet wide by maybe sixty feet long. The water would stay totally calm like that for about a minute until it would be broken by the gigantic gray back of an immense whale half again the size of our boat. He would rise to the surface, blow a spout of water and just as quickly sink back into the depths again for five or ten minutes when the water would regain an eerie calm and his back would rise again ever so slowsy to give us another water spout show. We were heading back by that time and beginning to be able to enjoy this kind of sight without the tension of indecision about where we were going.

> August 17 Thursday
> I was on watch about 6:30 AM when I noticed far off on the horizon the apparent shape of some ship coming our way. We were then going about a tenth of a knot trying to avoid drifting back into an island we had been trying to pass all night and half the day before. We were also positioned smack in the middle of a channel through which a fishing boat - the Lupita - had passed the evening before. We didn't even make an attempt to hail her - Bill needed us to help pass the shoals that we had been avoiding, although none of us ever spoke about that at the time. Partly because we thought we were so close to Panama, and partly because Carl and I felt somehow that Bill didn't want us to

leave him, no matter how many times he had said that we could get off if we wanted to (although later when we finally were being towed he told us that he couldn't let us get off, although he never explained why).

Anyway, when I saw that boat heading 290°, which was our bearing for Panama, and knowing that it could get to Panama in about 4 hours, and then perhaps we could fly out that evening, and be in Miami that same day, I got so excited I almost shouted!

What I actually did was to quietly call Carl using the hand over mouth technique - just like in a detective story - and we talked for a little while, me trying to convince him like mad to flag the boat down and see if we could get them to take us to Panama. At this point we were almost clear of the shoals and Bill, if left alone, would have relatively clear sailing, if the wind were to cooperate. So, everything looked right for a try to flag it down.

We didn't really know how to do it since we had tried a few days earlier to stop a coastal steamer (the only one we saw in the 3 days we had been laying off the coast) and failed. This time I got the megaphone and my bright red jacket and went forward and started waving like mad! I could see the crew on the deck wondering what was coming off, so I kept on waving frantically, trying to look as desperate as possible. Finally, FINALLY, and oh so prettily, the boat started swinging around and then came around all the way to near by us. By that time Carl and I had already dashed down and had our bags packed and ready to go. Then I passed the megaphone to Bill as the captain and told him to start talking. So he surprised me by instead of asking if they would take us on, he asked them how much it would cost to have them tow us to Panama because our motor had broken down.

They said that would not be necessary so we dragged up our two inch rope that we used as a sea anchor and tied it around the samson cleat, and got the other end to them by throwing a rope tied to it to them with a life preserver ring. When they started pulling us it was the greatest feeling to speed through the water like that. I had the mileage to Panama calculated down to about every minute's worth of traveling. That old tiller was terribly hard to hold going about 15 knots. Carl and I took half hour turns on it, straining our guts all the time, but eternally thankful to be heading so fast for Panama and terra firma! I was so glad to see the Panama City skyline that all I could do was just smile, and smile, and smile ...

The *Lupita* had so much power - it seemed to tow us like a toy, although the strain on the rope made me sure it was either going to pull the cleat off the boat or snap the rope which would then fly back and kill me and Fred serving poetic justice to the old man. It didn't anyway, and we made it back to Balboa in one piece. We called the Reynolds who came to pick us up and we bid farewell to our trusty captain. I think he hated us at that point but we could care less - we were so glad to be back on land again!

I have always hoped that Carl was more gracious in saying goodbye than I was. I just wanted to get away as fast as possible from that death trap Qui Viva and its possibly unhinged Capt. Queeg. I recall once glancing at him at the helm during a vicious storm, while Carl and I raced furiously about trying to put things in order. To give him his due,

The Lupita towing us to back to Panama

maybe it was just an expression of all-consuming concentration, but in the howling wind and rain it struck me as the fixed gaze of someone enjoying his last heroic moments as he rode his ship down into the deep. As we were finally leaving the boat, there was recollection of joyous moments and an unforgettable experience, but also dismay at such a poorly maintained vessel that had become a grave danger to all our lives: engine so poorly maintained that it didn't work, charts out of date, radio that didn't work, etc. Without a glance back, and stomping my foot on the first solid ground so hard that it hurt for a week, I just walked away with enormous relief from that source of a near, totally unnecessary watery grave for me and my friend.

The rest seems like so much nonsense - a customs mix-up, our re-entry papers to Panama, breakfast at the clubhouse, the foodsplit which we gave to the Reynolds, a couple of seat cancellations on the APA airline so we could get on a flight the next day, and a very ambivalent farewell to Bill Kaul who told us he thought that we had packed more sailing into the two and a half weeks we were with him than he had ever thought would have been possible (so, now, of course, we consider ourselves experienced sailors who have gone through the mill and know the ropes - we even began to remember to take up the boom rope when needed so that it wouldn't knock one of us overboard, which we had a hard time learning at first).

In the final count, the boom on the main mast had cracked, the mizzen mast was broken and could not hold its sail, the engine was barely able to run, the stove was in the ocean with the dinghy, and a hundred other things were makeshift repaired or damaged. The old Qui Viva was barely holding itself together. We were thankful we were able to make the last 50 miles towed behind a tuna boat out of Wilmington, Delaware, going to the Galapagos Islands that diverted its course just for our sakes. What a Godsend that boat was!

The summer was nearly over and we had only a week to get back to school. We looked at a world map and decided to fly into Miami and then hitch-hike back to San Diego. As the crow flies, Miami is closer to Panama than San Diego - that was a surprise to us.

CHAPTER 23 - The States

We boarded the airplane the next day and landed in Miami and kissed the tarmac. That was in the early afternoon, so we hopped on a municipal bus and asked the driver what bus to catch to get to California. He laughed and told us the city buses didn't go to California but he could tell us how to get to the west end of town, which he did. We followed his instructions and by dinnertime we were in a lower middle class suburb of Miami on the shoulder of a two-lane highway heading west.

We hitched a short ride to the next suburb and waited for a ride. We had been dropped off near a tavern on a two lane road, and, as we were "hitching" we kept walking slowly backwards in the direction that we were headed. We were still hiking when the sun went down. We had gotten about a hundred yards down the road from the tavern when we heard several people singing apparently as they left the tavern.

Then a car's brakes squeaked loudly and we heard a heavy "Thump!" Fred was still full of energy, so he left his bag with me and ran back to the tavern to see what had happened. By this time there were car headlights and taillights all around. I just sat by the side of the road on a little hump of a bank and waited. In five minutes Fred came running back with the story. A group of revelers had left the tavern and one of them who was particularly drunk had stumbled and fallen at the roadside and gotten his head run over. Fred didn't want to hitch-hike in the dark anymore that evening, so we hiked a couple hundred feet into the field alongside the road and rolled out our bags.

We got up the next morning early and started thumbing out on the highway again.

We got several rides and made a fairly uneventful trip up the west coast of Florida. The following afternoon we were picked up in Panama City, Florida, by a couple in a one or two year old beautiful white Cadillac. We asked the elderly couple why they stopped to pick up a couple of scrubs like us, because we looked pretty scruffy. The man said that in the 1930's he had to hitch-hike a lot and he always had sympathy for those who were out on the road. We told them our story and were very kind to us.

They felt badly about dropping us off but when we got to Mobile, Alabama, at about 5 PM we told them that my brother-in-law's father lived in Mobile and we were going to look him up and we would be fine. They left us off right in the middle of downtown Mobile and we started looking for a telephone.

We didn't want to use the corner public phone because it would use up some of our money - I had about $60 left, Fred had less - so we walked diagonally across the street to a very big old stone church. I knew my relative was active in some church, but I wasn't sure which one, and I knew his last name had to be Clarke because that was my brother-in-law's last name.

We went into the church and just started walking down a hallway. A lady met us and asked us what we were doing there; we explained our situation and she led us to an office and showed us a phone. I called several people with the last name of Clarke, but I didn't get anyone who knew my brother-in law. I didn't want to call home to ask for the name or phone number because I didn't want my family to know where I was - I wanted to arrive home as a surprise - and I knew that this relative was somewhat elusive and no one probably knew his phone number anyway.

As I was telephoning, Fred got engaged in a conversation with several of the church people about our trip and where we were going. They got interested and, when I had exhausted all possibility of finding my relative, Fred and a group of people were having a great conversation. One of them suggested that, if we couldn't find my relative, they would be pleased to have us speak at their church dinner.

That sounded fine to us, so they gave us a few minutes in the rest room to shave and wash our faces and then led us through the labyrinthine halls of the church to a set of double doors, which opened onto what looked like an immense room full of two or three hundred people. In between us and them were three tables lined up with place settings on them and we were directed to the head table to join the event. Before we had time to sit down, we were introduced as the guest speakers for the evening.

What a feed that was! All the spaghetti and garlic bread we could eat, and we stuffed ourselves. Then we got up and talked all about our trip for half an hour each, and they clapped and they laughed, and they got worried looks, and they were with us the whole time and we felt like their long lost children. When we were done, they mobbed us and wanted to know everything about us and more details about what we had done. What a great feeling! They loved us! We were the heroes of the moment even though I thought we looked like a couple of bums.

They were determined that we shouldn't go hungry, so they packed us a cake box full of spaghetti and a bread bag full of garlic bread. They showed us to a room in the basement where we could spend the night, so we un-rolled our bags and settled down to a very satisfied night's sleep.

The next morning we had more spaghetti for breakfast and started out on the road again.

Fred and I stayed together until that evening when we found ourselves in Jackson, Mississippi, at about nine o'clock. We were having awful lag periods between rides and we thought that maybe, if we split up, we might have more luck. Fred's right little toe had gotten infected on the boat and by this time about half of it was just a soggy, pussy, white looking mess, so he was especially anxious to get home to have his toe looked at.

When we landed in Miami, it was truly wonderful, kind of

like we had gotten out of jail, but we did then have a cross-country trek ahead of us, and I had just $5 left for the whole trip. And there weren't credit cards, etc., in those days, and I had no bank account of any kind. Because of my money issues again, I almost decided I couldn't afford to take the flight, but I couldn't see what any other options were. The Reynolds told us they didn't at all trust the Mexican airline that we were flying on, but we didn't really have a choice. My $5 had dwindled down to the grand total of 25¢ when we finally got to San Diego.

Because I had such little money as we were hitchhiking our way across the southern states, I was trying to make the spaghetti we had been given last as long as possible, but in the high heat and humidity I guess it went bad, and I got sick once, and threw up in a guy's car. I did manage to get my head out the window, but leaving a gruesome smear along the outside of the car.

When hitchhiking, there's always the question of where you sleep for the night. We slept in all manner of places, but I discovered on our way back across the country that a cornfield is a great place. It's quite sheltered, no one can see you, and there is room to stretch out your sleeping bag between the rows. However, one morning early I was suddenly awakened in a cornfield by a tractor, I guess, but it sounded like an army tank in full battle, about 2 feet away from me and apparently ready to squash the unseen visitor. I grabbed my stuff and dashed for the end of the field, but because the corn was so high, I never did see whatever startled me out of my sleep, and didn't hang around to find out.

To split up I just hiked down the highway a couple of

hundred yards, while Fred stayed where he was. Within half an hour a single guy pulled over to ask me where I was going. I told him "California" and he said "Great, hop in, I'm headed for L.A."

When I got in I asked him what he was going to do in L.A. and he just said he was going to try a business. I attempted to make some other conversation, but it went nowhere. As we sat together in the silent vehicle traveling along I began to get very sleepy. I asked him if he minded if I took a nap, and he said "No, as long as you can take over driving later on tonight." I told him I would and drifted off to a somewhat light sleep.

After a half an hour or so the fellow started chuckling these little chuckles. Then they got louder, and pretty soon he was just plain laughing. I wasn't too soundly asleep anyway, and when he started chuckling, I woke right up. I tried to let him know I was awake by my body movements, but finally I just began to feel uncomfortable and I asked him "What is it that's funny?"

He shut up immediately like a stone. I didn't say anything more and I attempted to get a little more sleep before my driving shift came. We drove on for another fifteen minutes or so and the chuckling began again; then laughing. With that kind of noise it was obvious I was awake, so I asked him again, "What's making you laugh?" "No, nothing..." was the reply.

The next time I didn't bother to ask. For the next few hours, every so often this fellow would just start chuckling and then laughing and then, all of a sudden, shut up. It gave me the willies. We ran out of gas at about 2:30 AM in the middle of a lot of farm land. There was no one else on the road. We pulled off on the shoulder as the car choked its last gasp and then we were stopped.

My driver didn't know what to do, so I volunteered to hike to the nearest farmhouse to see if they might give us some gas. I hiked about a mile and a half back toward Jackson to a farmhouse that was set back from the road behind a heavy bunch of hedges and trees. As I walked up to the door, the dogs inside started barking.

Several minutes passed before I saw a light inside; then I heard a voice inside asking "What do you want!" I told the voice "We ran out of gas...", and the voice told me to "Get the hell out of here if you know what's good for you!"

The voice sounded like it belonged to an older person, and I wasn't about to argue. I said "I'm sorry, I'll get out of here right now.... sorry I bothered you .. I'm leaving right now .... sorry...." I had the strangest feeling that someone was pointing a gun at me. In any case, I was not in any position to argue, so I didn't.

As I started for the next farmhouse, a moving van approached and I put my thumb out to hitch a ride. I couldn't believe it when that gigantic van pulled off on the side of the road and stopped. I ran up to the cab and told the driver what had happened. He was going in the same direction that I was so he told me to hop in and drove me back to the car.

My driver was impatiently waiting. When we pulled over the van driver offered us some gas, we just had to siphon it out of his tank. He had a can and a hose, so I offered to suck the gasoline into the hose. That's the first time I had ever done that, and I hope to never have to do it again. Gasoline is enough to make you gag!

Anyway, we siphoned out about a gallon of gas and poured it into our tank. My driver didn't even thank the truck driver; he was just sullen and quiet. I thanked him, but since I was just a kid along for the ride, I felt like the driver should have at least said something. He was just anxious and sullen about losing travel time by running out of gas. When we were ready to go he asked me to drive, so I took over. We woke up the owner of the next station we passed, and he kindly came out and filled up our tank.

I drove for about three or four hours, when he woke up again. At that point my uneasy bowels were ready to move so I told him I needed to stop the car. He okayed it and I jumped out and ran into a field about a hundred feet or so. It was almost dawn so there was a tiny bit of light in the sky and I had bad stomach cramps at that point. I spent five or ten minutes squatted down in that field, worrying whether he would drive off and leave me and take all my stuff, but he waited, and finally I got back in the car.

CHAPTER 24 - LONGVIEW AND HOME

> "We must welcome the future, remembering
> that soon it will be the past; and we must
> respect the past, remembering that once it
> was all that was humanly possible."
> G. Santayana

We drove into Longview, Texas, that morning at about 7 am. Out of the clear blue-sky my driver told me that he was going to get a motel room to get some sleep and that he wasn't going to go any further today. I told him "Fine, let me off here.." and he dropped me off in front of a nice looking, fairly new restaurant.

It was somewhat of a relief to get away from that guy because he had some very strange ways of acting - he didn't seem to want to talk at all about himself or what he was doing or exactly where he was going or why. Most people who pick up hitchhikers seem to enjoy talking; that guy seemed to be a real misanthrope. I was glad for an excuse to get away from him.

At that point in the trip I still had ten or fifteen dollars left - which made me feel pretty good. So I walked across the gravel parking area and into the local restaurant carrying my green duffle bag on my shoulder and looking like I hadn't had much of a night's sleep.

The restaurant was full of people of all kinds, talking a mile a minute and listening to country western music. I sat down at the counter and the waitress handed me a menu and wished me a "Good morning". I wished her the same, and began reading over the menu carefully.

A short stack of pancakes was $.75; milk and toast were $.25 each. When the waitress came back to ask me what I wanted I asked her how many pancakes were in a short stack and she said "Two". I asked her if I could just get one pancake because I was running low on money, and she took my order for one pancake and a small glass of milk.

I waited, and I waited, and I waited, and my order never seemed to come. Finally my waitress came back to my place carrying a big tray of food. I was anxiously looking over the tray to see if I could find my pancake and milk when she began unloading the whole tray in front of me! I was afraid she had mixed up my order with someone else's and I didn't have the money to pay for three pancakes, milk, hash browns, orange juice, sausages, eggs and coffee, so I blurted out "This must be for someone else!"

With a big smile she said, "This meal is compliments of the house. You eat all this good breakfast and enjoy it and be on your way." It's extraordinary how kind many people are.

"Thank.. thank you... thank you... this is really nice.... boy! I sure thank you all.. wow!" What a great breakfast that was. I owe Longview, Texas, for that one. I owe Mobile, Alabama, for the spaghetti. I owe a lot of people a lot for the whole trip!

My next ride took me into Dallas, Texas. I got there in the evening with no particular place to go and within a block of where I was dropped off there was a Salvation Army Mission. I know I had a distant relative somewhere in the area, but I didn't know any of her details, so I hiked over to the Mission and turned myself in.

I asked what I would have to do to stay there that night, and I was told that all I had to do was participate in a brief church meeting and sing a few hymns. For that I would get a bed to sleep in and a dinner and breakfast.

Dinner was a hot dog sandwich, and I enjoyed it. After dinner a bunch of the guys there and I went outside to sit around on the sidewalk and talk. I told them my story and some of them told me about their adventures train-hopping and otherwise bumming around. I got a good night's sleep and the next morning set off to hitchhike westward.

The new freeway going through town was only a few blocks from the Mission. I put my thumb out near the on-ramp and within minutes I was picked up - by a police car. The two policemen in the car asked me what I was doing there and I showed them a copy of the Balboa newspaper that had me and Fred on the cover telling the story of our travels. They enjoyed my stories so much that they offered to drive me to Fort Worth and to drop me off at a place where I would surely get a ride, which I did. Even the police are nice!

That ride took me to Abilene where I decided to walk the three blocks from the freeway to the closest grocery story to get some lunch- a box of Corn Pops and a quart of chocolate milk. I decided to take it with me instead of eating it there and I hiked out to the freeway, sat on a grassy bank and finished it all off.

As I took the last gulp of chocolate milk, I thumbed one of the few cars that went racing by. A hundred yards past me I saw that the car had hit its brakes and pulled over to a very hard stop on the highway shoulder. I started running as fast as I could with my big green bag bouncing against my back, trying to get to the car before they decided I was taking too long to reach them.

They waited, though, and as I approached, Fred leaned his head out of the back window and shouted "Hey BUM! Wher're you goin'?" Fred had gotten picked up by these three guys who were driving to California, and he just barely spotted me as they raced by me with my box of Corn Pops.

It was so good to see Fred again. His toe was looking worse than ever, but he said he was feeling fine.

We drove with those three cowboys to Nogales where they decided to go across the border to spend some time carousing. Fred and I weren't carousers, so we slept in the car until they got back. Then we took over and started driving West again. The next morning was dramatically beautiful on the desert. We drove for a while in a fairly dense fog. As we came up a hill, out of the fog, we could see that every plant on the desert was covered with a light frost and as the rising sun struck the plants the whole world before us looked like it was diamond studded. Our three hosts were asleep as we drove, but Fred and I really appreciated the beautiful views we saw.

We didn't go all the way to El Cajon with those guys. It seemed to us that they were basically thieving their way across the states, stealing anything they could get their hands on as they went. When Fred first got picked up by them, he made it clear to them that all he had left in his wallet was two dollars.

They dropped us off an hour or so before we would get to El Cajon telling us they wanted to go back to the town we had just passed through to do something. So they went back toward the town for maybe 100 yards, and then turned back around again in our direction and passed by us waving and laughing, happy apparently that they had left us standing on the road. Can't say I blame them for wanting to get rid of the extra baggage, but that little trick seemed fit in with their general characters.

The last guy who picked us up was an old guy in a beat up old pick up truck. I remember him well because although it was very hot, he wouldn't let me roll down the window whenever we were went through a town, because he was sure the cops would arrest us all if we had our arms out the window. We drove all the way to El Cajon with that guy, and got there around midday, a week before school was to start. I had them drop me off at the corner of Second Street and Pepper Drive, almost where my Mom had dropped us off to start the trip; Fred went on to Ross' house.

Ross was packing to get ready to start junior year at UCR and was ecstatic on seeing Fred. He had not heard from us for weeks and had seriously feared for our safety. Ross gave Fred a big bear hug but felt like he was hugging an empty suit because Fred had lost so much weight.

My folks and sisters were excited to see me and we had a happy reunion before I had to leave again for school. They were surprised a nineteen year old kid could do so many things without getting seriously sick or injured. I don't think we ever realized how fortunate we had been; we just started and ended the trip expecting things to ultimately work out.

Fred's toe healed just fine, he's married and has kids and grandkids now and lives somewhere in central Northern California - a retired college librarian and Information Technology Director. Ross married his college girl friend and named his first daughter Noemi. Our friend Noemi from Costa Rica came up a couple of times to visit with him and his family in California. The summer after the trip I volunteered for the Peace Corps and spent the following two years in Colombia, South America, before I finally came back to get my college degree.

CHAPTER 25 - FRIENDS

"One enemy is too many and a hundred friends too few."
Anonymous

Fred, Ross, and I have loosely kept in touch since THE TRIP. In 2016, more than fifty years afterwards, we got together for a little Trip Reunion in Carlsbad, California, where Ross still lives. He and his wife prepared a sumptuous meal for us with all kinds of fresh garden vegetables. We had a great time remembering the events of the past and bringing each other up on our lives today. We continue to appreciate each other almost as we did in those early days, and we wished each other well as we face the challenges of children, grandchildren and the changing tides of the world. I never would have made THE TRIP without Fred; and, if it hadn't been for Ross' assertiveness at a critical point along the way, Fred and I never would have made it to Panama.

Carl, Carla, Ross, Fred in Ross' dining room April 29, 2016

Carl, Ross, Fred on Ross' front lawn, April 2016

REFLECTIONS

"Be happy for this moment. This moment is your life."
Omar Khayyam

Some closing thoughts about THE TRIP from each of us:

FRED
For the three of us, "The Trip" impacted our lives, but I think for each of us differently. I do know that for me, I came to value my two traveling companions even more as we faced various difficulties. Ross stepped in, as he really often had like during our "crisis", to help in a time of need. I had always genuinely looked up to Carl, but experiencing the stresses of the sometimes life and death situations that occurred during our little sea jaunt, made me aware of and value even more his calm confidence and strength of character.

I think we all would say we had positive life experiences that have affected us even until now. The various challenges on our journey, including those on the Qui Viva, reinforced in my recognition the fragility and brevity of life and the deeper value of spiritual, non-temporal matters.

There was an interesting spiritual aspect to our friendship that was somewhat unusual. I had been raised in a very religious environment, but by the time my freshman year started, I had become very disillusioned and disenchanted with my childhood religion, and I was moving rapidly toward agnosticism. Ross was one of those who helped me find a loving, vital Christian fellowship where the teachings and spirit of Jesus are a reality, and this has been an absolute joy and an anchor to me for my whole life. Ross himself, however, later moved to the atheist camp, while Carl left that persuasion for the Church of Jesus Christ of Latter Day Saints. So, we were a kind of motley mix of moving parts, but that never seemed to interfere with our friendship or mutual respect. Our interest in philosophy, belief systems and political ideas seemed to bond us rather than separate us.

There are, on the other hand, many factors that do tend to separate people. During our trip, we experienced firsthand that sociological concept of the "other". Aspects like race, geography, income, religion, appearance, culture, capability, language, etc., etc. often create a sense of "us" and "them". Those who don't share familiar characteristics usually are looked upon as different, as the "other". Differences can be accepted, but quite often the others are kept at a distance, or even mistrusted, misunderstood, feared, etcetera.

Our travels took us through countries with obvious similarities, but also real differences in history, culture, values, etc., and we recognized this concept of the "other" multiple times during our trip. Before we started, our friends in the United States cautioned us to be careful in Mexico because "it could be dangerous". This warning was earnestly repeated at every single crossing we made into another country. Whether it was Guatemala, Honduras, Nicaragua, Costa Rica, etc., I heard the same caveat about the next country: BE CAREFUL THERE. While that was well intentioned, and often not bad advice, what we found, however, as Carl notes, was overwhelmingly a welcoming, friendly, generous humanity out there ready to be helpful to some pretty naïve, young, adventurous guys.

We learned quite a few lessons on our trip, and an important one was to try to respect not just the "us" but also the "them". Since one of the most powerful messages in human history was "love your enemies", trying to carry a message similar to that in our hearts toward all was a valuable lesson for me.

ROSS
I remember that Fred felt so bad about the poverty he saw that he did not want to buy things for his house after he married. After retiring, he and Sally realized his high school ambition of becoming a missionary. He spent time in the Ukraine helping the church grow there. The twist was Carl converted to the Church of Jesus Christ of Latter Day Saints from atheism and I became an atheist.

The greatest effect on my life was the friendships that I made in Costa Rica. I was enamored of Noemi Alvarado and fascinated with her mother Luisa de Alvarado. Noemi visited my family about three years after the trip. Then Luisa came to stay with us for about six months. She was a great source of Spanish language learning. She loved to tell stories and jokes. She told the same jokes over and over making us laugh and cry. She should have been a standup comedian! The good thing was that she did not want to learn English because she thought she would not ever be able to tell stories and jokes as well in English as she did in Spanish.

A few years after The Trip Walfrid Alvarado, Assistant Treasurer of the National Bank of Costa Rica, made us a visit. He and I took a short trip to the Grand Canyon.

An adopted son of the Alvarado's, Paco Alvarado, visited for a few months, and a family friend, Marcos Saenz, stayed in our home for a six month visit. I delivered Marcos to Canada where he over-stayed his visa and was returned to Costa Rica. He became a Costa Rican banker and raised a family.

I have followed the lives of the Alvarado family for years, and communicate with them still. Freddy Alvarado, Noemi's brother, has a Facebook page. Noemi's daughter who lives in

Argentina is a friend on Facebook, as are several other family members.

I have made five trips to Costa Rica. Once, years after our trip, we visited Tobias Cordero, who is now the owner of a large trucking company. He took us to his private jungle in Sarapiqui, Costa Rica, just north of San Jose.

The familiarity with language and customs that I developed from this continued contact with those we met on the trip helped me in my career as an elementary school teacher.

Ross' Bachelor's Degree

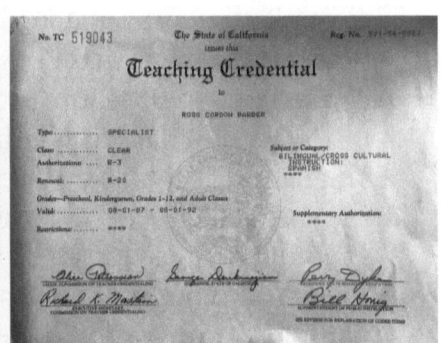
Ross' Teaching Credential

Ross' Master's Degree

It influenced my decision to pursue a Master's Degree in Education, and helped me become a fully certified multi-cultural bilingual educator, able to work in all school levels, kindergarten through adult.

Before completing my Master's Degree in 1976, I took my young family on a six month driving trip through Mexico where I stayed with a family that I knew from my teaching, and with a family with three teachers whom I had met in a Zacatecan teachers' convention.

The trip with Carl and Fred greatly influenced my vocational choice and my desire to spend a lot of time in Mexico and Central America.

I, too, finally made it to Panama when we visited Panamanian friends there. We went to Isla Barro Colorado, a nature preserve; then crossed the isthmus on a train.

Ross' Certificate of Competence in Spanish

I have thoroughly enjoyed the experiences that the trip with Carl and Fred led to in my life. Sometimes I say "I am a wannabe Mexican". By many I am called "Don Rosendo".

CARL
Until the trip I had a vague feeling that people were basically pretty good and could be trusted to be kind and do the right thing. After the trip I knew that was true and I built my future upon that knowledge. Thank you all who helped us along the way and made our trip possible. You helped me understand what a joy it is to have faith in my fellow man, and to have the strength to act on that faith. What great people you are! What a wonderful world we live in!

ABOUT THE AUTHORS

Carl Stephani, ICMA-CM, is a Credentialed Manager and Life Member of the International City/County Management Association (ICMA), and the American Planning Association (APA). He studied at the University of California at Riverside, the University of New Mexico, Columbia University, and the Georgetown University School of Foreign Service; and he holds a Bachelor's Degree in Social Science from the University of California at Berkeley and a Master's Degree in Regional Planning from the Maxwell School of Citizenship and Public Affairs of Syracuse University. Marilyn Stephani holds a Bachelor's Degree in Biology from Wheaton College in Norton, Massachusetts, completed graduate work in plant physiology at Syracuse University, and has been a licensed Realtor®.

Carl and Marilyn have consulted in planning in Arizona, New Mexico, and Colorado. During his more than 40 years of professional work, Carl has held the positions of planning director, town manager, city councilman, and county commissioner in various local governments in New York, California, Oregon, Colorado, Arizona, and Connecticut. He also served as a United States Peace Corps volunteer in Bogota, Colombia; a Peace Corps trainer at the University of Missouri and Vanderbilt University; a New York City Urban Fellow; and a United Nations intern.

Carl and Marilyn were born and raised in the state of New York, and now reside in Tulsa, Oklahoma.

If you enjoyed this book, please enter your positive comments about it in a review on www.amazon.com or another internet book review web site. You may also enjoy the following other books written by Carl and Marilyn:

ON BECOMING A CITY MANAGER
A Chronicle of Intrigue and Deception

ZONING 101
A Practical Introduction

PLANNING CITIES 101
A Practical Introduction

You can contact the authors at:
carl@carlstephani.com

I've heard tell of a proof
That says you'll never
Always be happy,
And it made me glad
To hear it told that way.